LAURIE,

THANK YOU!

SELLER MISTAKES

What You Were Never Told About Selling Your Home and Why it Should Matter to You

Michael B. Bell

Published by Best Seller Publishing®, St. Augustine, FL
Best Seller Publishing® is a registered trademark.
Printed in the United States of America.
ISBN: 978-1-956649-07-9

For more information, please write:
Best Seller Publishing®
53 Marine Street
St. Augustine, FL 32084
or call 1 (626) 765-9750
Visit us online at: www.BestSellerPublishing.org

SELLER MISTAKES

What You Were Never Told About Selling Your Home
and Why it Should Matter to You

Michael B. Bell

TABLE OF CONTENTS

INTRODUCTION

For most people, including real estate agents, selling a home is complicated and frustrating because of one reason: mistakes. In this book I will show you how to make the most money by avoiding these common mistakes. What's sad is that most agents don't really want you to know about them—because these mistakes often work to THEIR advantage, not yours.

This book is intended for all home sellers, especially those who have struggled to sell their homes. This book is about what *works* to sell your home. It doesn't matter if the market is going up or down, in transition, or in a pandemic. I will also cover what *seems* to work but doesn't—and why.

Everything you'll read in this book is simple, backed by a lot of statistics, and based on common sense.

When a sale goes sideways, or nowhere at all, homeowners often agonize about what they should have done differently. Maybe you're thinking, "This book is going to explain the importance of curb appeal, the importance of pricing your home based on other sales, how to make the right improvements, decluttering, staging, and posting on the Multiple Listing Service (MLS)." These strategies are all important and very basic, and you likely already know all of them. But this book covers everything else—most of which agents won't tell you about.

What are these crucial issues? I'll cover the pros and cons of several elements of home-selling that most sellers know little about. Things like:

- *acronym inflation*
- *boutiques and international brokerages*
- *brokers license vs. sales license*
- *commissions*
- *dual agency*
- *FSBO-ing*
- *the For Sale sign*
- *hiring friends and family*
- *industry dynamics*
- *networks*
- *open houses*
- *picking agents to interview*
- *pricing*
- *print ads*
- *theft*
- *working with teams*

Also, I'll deal with firing your agent.

Do I have your attention yet?

After reading this book, I can promise that you'll experience a smoother selling process and, more importantly, secure the best price for your home.

■ ■ ■

Before I decided to write this book, my wife, Anne, asked me if anyone else had written anything like it. We both assumed there would be at least one book already published. But we couldn't find it. The only other house-selling-related books that we could find described things like explaining the sales process or discussing the basics of investing. The rest were written by agents reliving their successes and fun life experiences. Some just liked to brag. Because, if you know what's in these pages, it doesn't *help the agent*.

Because very little of this book helps the agent.

Why is this the first time you're hearing this kind of advice? Agents rely on the customs of the real estate industry that have developed over a long time, and too often these customs get in the way of what's actually *best for the home seller*.

Here's the lowdown:

To get more listings, an agent is

> **SELLER MISTAKE**
> Not realizing that most agents are focused on using sellers and their houses to benefit themselves and their brokerages, not their sellers.

trained to handle three simple questions that a seller usually asks. The agent knows they need to have good answers to:

1. How much money will I get when my house sells?
2. How fast can I sell my house?
3. Will this agent do the best job for me?

We all know the agent needs to address these questions to get your listing. And therein lies the rub: *their answers often lead you astray*. By understanding this, and the dynamics of the industry as laid out in this book, you will be able to better evaluate what's best for *you*, not your agent.

Not only will homeowners benefit from this book, but so will real estate agents—particularly those interested in building thriving, successful businesses based on trust, referrals, and repeat business. Agents don't need to be completely self-serving to succeed! It's crucial to find an agent who is always going to put your best interests first.

HOW DID I COME UP WITH THIS STUFF?

This book references a variety of sources. Most are from the National Association of Realtors® (NAR), a large trade group founded in 1908 that now has over 1.4 million members that's among the largest political action committees (PAC). Funded by real estate agents, it is the number two spender on lobbying in the United States, only after the U.S. Chamber of Commerce. As you read through this book, keep in mind that a PAC's primary purpose is to influence public policy in the direction most favorable to the group's *members*. NAR's clients are Realtors®—pure and simple. Realtors'® clients are home buyers and sellers. Therefore, NAR's clients are *not* home buyers and sellers.

For over forty years, NAR has sent out a survey to recent homebuyers, many of whom also sold a home. The survey uses a random sample that is weighted to represent home sales geographically. The result is a data-rich report that outlines market characteristics and describes the demographics of home buyers and sellers. Statistical changes in buyer and seller behaviors from year to year are rarely significant, so this data will be highly relevant even if it's years old. There are few other significant sources or surveys about real estate. I've done my best to scour for more, but most of my stats are from NAR. Unfortunately, and sadly, there is no better source for residential real estate industry statistics.

Since I happen to be a member of NAR, I requested a copy of their survey. To my surprise, I was denied. I was told that in order to see it, I'd need to be one of the randomly selected 160,000 recipients. So I decided to work my connections. It actually took me two months to get a copy. Now, I can't reveal my sources—they told me if I did, that I'd be found in a ditch. (They were joking. But they did ask that I not publish how I received the information.)

In this book I dive into the most common industry customs, how these customs are promoted, and the statistics (or lack of statistics) that no one talks about. After reading *Seller Mistakes*, you can decide for yourself if the customs and what NAR promotes benefit the homeowner, or are skewed to help the agent win more business at your expense, over and over again.

But before I get into all of that, I'd like to share a little bit about me, my family, and my journey in the real estate industry.

HOW I ENDED UP SELLING HOUSES

To start, I grew up in Southern California, the middle of three boys. Both sides of my family were in sales all their lives. My mother's family built hundreds of homes in the 1970s, and my father sells life insurance. They worked hard. Learning from my parents, my brothers Bryen, Darren, and I always worked hard, too. We started working when we were 11 years old: we worked paper routes, sold programs and souvenirs at Dodger Stadium, mowed lawns, dug holes—whatever we could do to make a buck. Each of us participated in Scouts, where we learned to "Be Prepared," and earned our Eagle Scout awards.

After graduating in finance from Gonzaga University, I worked a couple of office jobs that required a real estate sales license. I serviced and managed commercial loans for the most part. My stepfather, Ron, was a general contractor, so I also worked part-time on construction sites while taking a course at Pasadena Community College where we built a home from scratch. I did everything from digging the foundation and reading the plans to installing the faucets and meeting the inspectors.

At twenty-four years old, I decided I wanted to flip homes. I was happy when my grandfather Tony Paneno, a retired home builder, agreed to finance me. It took a full year to find my first house: a two-bedroom Fannie Mae foreclosure on Marengo Avenue in Pasadena, California. The year was 1997, the asking price was $89,000, and we were in a buyer's market. I offered $82,500 cash and the bank accepted. As you might imagine, I was thrilled. I fixed everything in that house with my own two hands. And then I sold the home for $122,000. After expenses, my profit was $16,000. I was elated. Success!

In the next few years, I went on to flip twenty different homes. Knowing what I know now, I made a lot of mistakes, mostly with the sales process. But I still at least made money.

Usually I bought directly from the listing agent on the property. This was almost always an uncomfortable experience. I never understood how they could fairly represent both buyer and seller at the same time. Still, I always got good deals. More on that later....

I almost never liked how my home sales were handled. I always wound up working with the wrong agents who didn't have the right strategies. To me, the process seemed too self-serving for the agent. Here's what I mean. Most agents started the marketing process by bringing their own buyers before going on the open market (what's up with that?). Open houses were always a must (why?). And almost everything they did was sloppy. The "For Sale" signs were crooked, their flyers were uninspired, and the photos were dull. Worst of all, they didn't even know their way around a contract.

So I finally decided to get my real estate broker's license. That way, I could take control and actually represent myself. But (full disclosure), I never really wanted to be an agent. Why? Well, to be honest, I didn't like most agents. It didn't seem to me to be an admirable career.

But then something happened. After I got my license, the neighbors of my flipped properties started asking me if I could help them sell their homes. I met other people who asked me to help them buy and sell. Then I got even more exciting requests: agents started asking if they could join me, since I was a successful broker. I was going in a new direction, and it was time to sell the trucks and the wheelbarrow.

The business of flipping homes had been a rollercoaster of emotions and hard on me and my finances. I discovered that I no longer had the stomach for it. So, I started to transition from flipping homes to becoming the youngest practicing broker in town, with my own brokerage office.

Bradmont Realty was born. It grew to ten agents strong. In case you are wondering, the name "Bradmont" comes from a combination of Bradley, my middle name (and the name of my firstborn), and "mont," for mountains. Diehard Boy Scouts who have heard of Philmont, the Scout ranch in New Mexico, will understand the inspiration behind the name.

I moved from my dining-room table to an office on the top floor of Arcade Lane in Pasadena. With a successful brokerage I never worked harder in my life, and I was very proud. However, having a boutique office with a small network was tough. A great website, a nice office, a slick presentation, a good number of producing agents, and my shiny smile would only take me so far.

In 2000, during this transition from flipping to selling, I met my future wife, Anne, and I realized that she was the girl for me. A few years later, I sold my brokerage to a national brand, we married, and went on to have two beautiful boys. From there I entered pure sales, and I have never looked back.

Since then, in the past twenty years, I have sold more than 500 homes. I've represented judges, attorneys, mediators, movie stars, CEOs, banks, foreign nationals, charities, Caltech scientists, Realtors®, executors, developers, trustees, nonagenarians, one prisoner, and many priests. I was fortunate enough that The Wall Street Journal has ranked me in the top 0.1% real estate agents in the nation. As the top seller at Sotheby's International Realty in Pasadena for the last six years, my clients consistently tell me that they love my approach. That's why I'm sharing it with you. I want you to know the secrets and the mistakes—the behind-the-scenes things that actually make a difference in selling your home.

I believe that this book is going to be so great for you! Look at it like a cheat sheet, a way to hack the real estate system to your benefit. After reading this book, I am confident that you will understand how to sell your home without mistakes.

—Mike

1

GIVING YOUR LISTING AWAY

It always baffles me when a seller says they *gave* their home listing to someone. That's how a lot of sellers hire their agent—by *giving* it to them. They say, "I gave the listing to Mark," "I gave it to my friend," "I gave it to my wife's college friend." To me, the word *gave* means that the agent didn't need to work for it and the seller didn't see the value a really good agent brings to the table. I hope to convince you that this single principle, that the agent should earn your business, is paramount.

Nobody says they *gave* their kidney operation to a doctor. They say that they picked Dr. Greene for very specific reasons; that doctor earned the right to be selected. Dr. Greene was the expert. It was a decision based on professional qualifications more than anything else.

No, no, no, no, no. Don't ever give your home listing to an agent. That's what most sellers do. And most sellers regret it. I can't tell you how many times I've heard a homeowner say, "I *gave* my listing to Joe or Sally." It's as if sellers think that all agents are created equal, that we all do the same thing, that we all push the same buttons, and it doesn't matter who's hired; the result will be the same anyway. This is the first and most common seller mistake.

> **SELLER MISTAKE**
> Not making your agent *earn* your listing.

If your agent *earns* it, you will be rewarded with the best possible outcome: the highest sale price possible in the shortest amount of time with minimal headaches. This book is about making your agent *earn* your business by doing what's best for you.

For me, I always ask my sellers to allow me to *earn* their listing.

After reading this book, with statistics and simple common sense on your side, you will have the upper hand in the agent hiring process.

I mentioned earlier the National Association of Realtors® has done a lot of research. Of all NAR stats that I found, these are the most impactful to my points:

- *75% of all sellers don't interview more than one agent to sell their house,*

- *Only 10% of sellers interview three or more agents, and*

- *75% of all sellers don't use the same agent on their next transaction.*

When I first saw these statistics, I thought, "There is no way these numbers could be correct." However, the data doesn't lie. Let's think this through. First, there are a huge number of agents in the marketplace. Of course, some are very good and very successful. But the reality is that most aren't. I've been selling for over twenty years. I've experienced the first two stats (that most sellers don't interview more than one agent and only a few interview three or more agents), but I've not experienced the last one (most sellers don't use the same agent on their next transaction).

As I considered these startling figures, I started to think about the 80/20 rule (the Pareto principle) and how it applies to this business. The Pareto principle is a consistent rule stating that 80% of the effects come from 20% of the causes. That's why they call it the 80/20 rule. To say it another way, *80% of the sales are done by 20% of all agents, and 20% of all agents handle 80% of all sales.* The principle says to focus on the efforts of the top 20% to maximize your result. If you dig further into our industry data, you'll find that our business is skewed even more. It's actually 10% of the agents do 90% of the business. Now, to be clear, I'm not suggesting that you try to find an agent in the top 20%, or even in the top 10%, because I think you can do even better than that. I recommend that you focus on the top 1% to 2%. You want an agent who does such a great job that you use them again. Right?

Most agents can be categorized as "satisfactory." You might find someone good, but not great. If you've bought and sold your home at least twice, you are undoubtedly nodding your head in agreement. As my real estate coach constantly says, "Good is the enemy of great." I love that expression. So many people settle on good and give their listing to the first agent they talk to. But does that get you *great* results?

A great agent is worth every penny of their commission. A bad or mediocre agent will almost always cost the seller money and create liability issues, many of which can haunt that seller for years. However, an excellent agent will almost always make a seller the most amount of money in the shortest possible time, with the fewest headaches. I hate to say it: you get what you pay for. It all starts with how the agent handles the commission negotiation. I'll go more into this in Chapter 7.

And, unfortunately, I have more bad news: finding a top agent doesn't mean that they won't take you down Mistake Lane. Some are top agents because they are extremely good at what serves their own goals, not their clients. Also, don't worry too much about hiring someone who might seem to be too busy. Most top agents know how to make it happen. That's why they are on top.

The research clearly shows that most sellers simply don't pick the right agent. There are several reasons for this.

- People are in a hurry to get the business of buying or selling completed.

- Time spent with several agents seems like time wasted when all they need is one agent.

- Sellers think that if their neighbor sold a house with Jack, then Jack can sell their house, too. All agents are alike, aren't they? Nice people in nice clothes who know how to sell?

No. Spending time researching agents is never a waste of time. Omitting this step is one of the biggest seller mistakes. A top agent who is your advocate will help you avoid errors, so the more time you spend researching agents, the happier you will be with the outcome. The goal is to hitch your wagon to a bright and shining star. It isn't that daunting of a process; this is the first of many steps to put the odds in your favor.

First, I strongly recommend to consider only local agents. You are almost always at a disadvantage if you work with people in real estate who aren't in your area. They don't know the trends, the neighborhoods, the houses, or even the local agents. Don't worry: every single area has top agents. You just need to spend a little time finding them. It isn't as easy as searching "Top Agents, Anytown, USA." You will quickly find that many agents pay for placement on these lists. Don't buy the hype!

HOW TO FIND TOP AGENTS TO INTERVIEW

1. Call the managers at the top local brokerages and ask who their top two agents are. Don't hire a manager, because they tend to be part-time agents who primarily spend time dealing with other people's problems.

2. Search online for lists in your area; be careful about trusting a list that agents pay to be on.

3. Ask friends, family, and neighbors.

Gather five to ten names and start researching them. Pick at least three whose names appear often, who demonstrate experience and success. Their production numbers should be easy to find and you will find their properties on multiple web platforms. And while you're checking online, see whether an agent's name appears for doing something great, stupid, or even illegal. And make sure you have the names right. Apparently, there are no fewer than thirteen Mike Bells selling real estate out there!

Now that you have your list, the next step is to call as many as five of the agents who have made the cut. You don't need to give them your contact information or your home address. You can describe your location, size, and condition so they can get a better idea about your listing. Realize that this phone call is not about finding out what your home is worth. Rather it's about finding out if the agent is the *right fit* for you.

Make sure to tell each of them that the agent you intend to hire needs to *earn* your business, and that you aren't just going to give it away. These are trigger words for a top agent, so listen to what they say. Let the agent know that you plan to interview several agents, and that you will let them know if they are one of the top three. Each call doesn't need to last more than ten minutes. Chat with them and see if there's good chemistry. You could be working with your agent for months, so it helps if you get along well.

Now is the time to ask point blank what they will do to sell your home and what makes them different from the other agents. Take notes while you are chatting with them. Most will want to meet with you as soon as possible because they are trained to set an appointment. Don't fall for it.

Once you pick your top three, call them back. Let them know they have competition. Give them your contact information and your address. And, by the way, you don't need to mention that you have the ultimate seller hack, this book, in your possession.

> **SELLER MISTAKE**
>
> Not interviewing at least three agents before hiring one.

A good agent will ask what's important to you. Let that person know that you want to sell for the most amount of money, and you don't want your agent to make any mistakes. Don't tell the agents what you think your price should be, and don't tell them what the mistakes might be. You don't need to bring up the commission question unless they bring it up. Save that for later.

While you are talking to multiple agents, you might find that they sound the same. If an agent can't explain or effectively show you their value proposition or they don't hit on the main subjects in this book, then move on.

Too often a seller decides on an agent because of the fee they charge, specifically how low it is. I have a full chapter that covers this, but it is worth addressing it now. If you give the principles in this book a chance, you will find that many of the higher-fee agents have more success for their clients and earn more for them than discount agents. Don't use the commission as a deciding factor yet.

Once you've gone through this book's various topics and feel comfortable that a certain agent has earned your business, here are a few things to keep in mind.

Ask the agent what the best marketing practices are for your situation. Over the phone you can describe your home, or take photos or do a video conference to get more specific. The best marketing practices depend on things like if it's a buyer's market (more than six months of inventory), a seller's market (less than six months of inventory), the condition of the home, upgrades, and if the home will be sold as-is, fixed up, vacated, or staged. Ask them if your home will be on the MLS. Ask what kind of advertising will be done, and if there will be a focus on digital marketing. Ask for examples of other properties they've sold. With the knowledge gleaned from this book, you will know quickly if they're going to take you down Mistake Lane. Keep reading; there's a lot to this book.

Also ask your agent how they'll keep you informed. Do you want updates via email, text, or phone, and how often? I've had clients who asked me not to give them any update unless it's good news. Other clients want to know the nitty-gritty of everything. Let your agent know that NAR says the number one complaint consumers have about their agent is that there isn't enough communication.

Ask if you will be able to be let out of the contract if you are unhappy. I cover this in the last chapter. It may not be in writing, but if the licensed agent gave you their word, then you should count on it.

■ ■ ■

THE NAME GAME:
BROKER, SALESPERSON, REALTOR®?

There are a lot of different names in real estate. So, when you sell your home, should you hire a broker, a salesperson, or a Realtor®? What's the difference?

Most agents have a basic salesperson's license. Usually, the more experienced agents have a broker's license. There are two kinds of brokers: the designated broker, who is usually the manager, and then there are agents like me who decided to get the more difficult license. Perhaps they have had their own brokerage, were in management, or went on their own at one time. These folks are called a broker-associate or an associate-broker. A broker's license requires years of proven sales experience and passing a test that is twice as long and hard as the salesperson's license test. Unlike the salesperson's exam, the failure rate for the broker license is high.

There are over two million licensed agents in the United States; only about 65% of them are Realtors®. To be a Realtor®, you must be a licensed salesperson or broker who pays NAR dues and subscribes to their strict code of ethics. The word Realtor® is trademarked by NAR and is a professional title for its members to distinguish them from outsiders. So, a real estate agent can be a broker or a salesperson, and a Realtor® if they pay their NAR dues.

IS IT BETTER TO HIRE A REALTOR®?

Consumers say yes. In 2018 (the year with the most recent data available), the California Association of Realtors® (CAR) asked consumers what was important to them in selecting an agent. "Referrals from people I trust" garnered the highest response at 69%. Referrals are also the number one source of business for almost every top agent. The next important item in selecting an agent was "finding agents who had listings like my home" (64%), followed by "looking at websites with ratings of agent's performances" (62%). In fourth place was "having a personal relationship with the agent." Interestingly, "belonging to a Realtor® organization" came next, at 52%.

If you like to play the odds, hire an agent with the highest license available (a broker license), and one who's a Realtor®.

ACRONYM INFLATION

While you've been focusing on what type of license the agent has, and if they're a Realtor® or not, you will undoubtedly notice a number of designations that are meant to convey expertise.

We've all seen the agent business card with a long trail of abbreviations. For the big offenders we call it acronym inflation. The designations are very popular with real estate agents. I even have a few. They just don't necessarily make me a better agent.

Agents get inundated with educational opportunities from NAR, CAR and their state associations. Topics and their acronyms include: GREEN Designation, working with seniors (SRES®), working with first-time buyers (FTBS), and regular buyers (ABR®), working with large landowners (ALC), international buyers (CIPS), diversity sensitivity (AHWD), working with sellers (SRS), resort sales (RSPS®), short sales and foreclosures (SFR® and CDPE), general practice (GRI, CRS, LREB, and CRE®), probate (CPS and PPS), disaster preparedness (DPK), office management (OMC), assistant manager (CRB, IREM, and RCE), team leadership (TLC), smart homes (SMART), marketing (MIRM), real estate teams (C-RETS), digital marketing (e-PRO), property management (PMM and CMP®), performance management (PMN), military relocation (MRP), pricing strategy (PSA), negotiations (RENE), and on and on. Whew! When it comes to these acronyms, realize that the coursework is usually great, and most of the students are newer or unsuccessful agents.

When I first entered the real estate business, I had a lot of extra time and not a lot of clients. I wanted to make money, but I also wanted to learn as much as I could as quickly as possible. Some courses average 50 hours, like my Graduate, Realtor® Institute (GRI) and my California Probate Specialist (CPS) designations. My Seniors Real Estate Specialist® (SRES®) designation took 12 hours, which I received online during the first month of the pandemic lockdown. We all had downtime.

SELLER MISTAKE

Relying too much on acronyms behind the agent's name.

According to NAR, 72% of brokerages encourage their agents to get more education because it reduces brokerage liability. Occasionally, you will find an agent with a lot of experience and acronyms. But they are far and few between. It doesn't mean they can handle the transaction like an experienced broker. Don't let yourself get too hung up on titles.

We've covered the basics: interview at least three local experienced agents, gravitate to those who have a broker's license and are Realtors®, and don't get too hung up on their acronyms. Focus on their experience and know-how. 75% of all sellers don't approach it this way.

You could stop here and you might be okay. However, the advice in this book gets better and better. Not only will you be able to cut through the process faster and know more than most agents, but you're also probably going to sell your home for the highest amount of money possible. It all starts by signaling to the agents that you aren't going to *give* your home listing away.

Take a moment and say to yourself: the next agent I hire will *earn* my business. The next time you sell a home and you have a good experience with the agent, be sure to tell your friends that the agent earned your business—you didn't give away your home listing. I guarantee that with this simple task in mind you will have a much better experience.

2

NOT ALL AGENTS ARE CREATED EQUAL

The good news and the bad news is that getting into real estate has a low barrier to entry. Almost anyone can get a license, and that's intentional because it's a tough business and most fail quickly.

If our business were easy, everyone would be doing well, and no one would be dropping out. This career isn't for everyone, and the failure rate is high. According to NAR, 87% of all new agents are out of the business within five years. They fail. To say it differently, when you hire someone with five or fewer years under their belt, you are hiring someone with an 87% chance of failure! Ouch!

Many agents don't make much money. Most earn below the federal poverty level. According to NAR, the median income for an agent is $50,000. About a decade ago the California Department of Real Estate considered making the exams more difficult. But they punted. The reasoning was because, "real estate sales is an excellent occupation for someone without a high school education." What? Also, the industry needs a steady flow of new agents.

Today, the salesperson's test is not very difficult. Most pass, in part because the state is flooded with hundreds of test prep companies and online education courses. It's a big business. The 2021–2022 budget for the California Department of Real Estate is $56 million. This industry simply needs more and more people. Part of the reason is that people leave the business in droves. Most brokerages have a revolving door, and they recruit constantly. New agents are always coming in, while other agents are quitting. NAR says that 15% of its membership turns over every year.

It's always been this way. For those who can succeed, it's a fantastic career. Although barriers to entry are low, the barriers to success are high.

In California, a licensee doesn't need a high school diploma. Applicants need only to pass the General Education Development (GED) exam. Misdemeanors and even a few felonies are allowed. All of the educational prerequisites can be done online, and the test prep companies guarantee a passing grade of 70%.

According to NAR, only 31% of all agents in the U.S. hold a bachelor's degree and 13% hold a graduate degree or higher. Translation: more than half the agents out there don't have a college degree. Here in California, a college degree is important. CAR's most recent survey says 78% of consumers said an agent's educational background was either "extremely important" or "very important" in their decision to hire. I'm glad to hear that. Keep in mind, that many people don't even realize that their agent might not be college educated.

According to NAR surveys, only 21% of home sellers can even remember the first name of their last real estate agent. This makes sense because often a better agent comes into focus, most agents don't stay in contact, and real estate agents leave the business in droves. Did I mention there is a lot of burnout and turnover in our industry?

There are also a number of part-time agents who are also appraisers, property managers, or loan officers. I've worked with so many of these part-timers over the years and have yet to find a single one who's a top agent. It's just tough to be tops in any profession when you have two or more professions.

> **SELLER MISTAKE**
>
> Choosing an agent who is not fully committed to their real estate career.

A jack of all trades is a master of none. Stick with a full-time experienced sales agent.

ROOKIES IN THE BUSINESS

If you're a rookie agent and reading this, I apologize. You probably feel like I'm recommending that no one hire you. But there's no need to worry. With over five million home sales in the United States every year, and

75% of sellers interviewing only one agent, the odds are in your favor. My advice is to stay at it, contact as many people as you can, sharpen your skills, be of service, and learn these strategies. You will build a great business.

I actually love working with rookie agents because they're usually starving for a commission, and they will drive far for it. They're easy to spot. You can hear it in their voices when they call. They'll often tell the listing agent: "I'm so tired of driving. I need to get my buyer into a house badly, and this is how high I can get them to go."

I like to ask them how high or low their client will go. There's nothing wrong with asking that question. However, it's probably unethical and a breach of their agency to tell me. But they still usually do. Sometimes the agent just wants to get the transaction done, so they'll tell you way too much about their buyer.

Even though rookies usually don't last, brokerages love new agents. They know that a brand-new agent is good for a few transactions. Most new salespeople got into the business with the promise of a friend or family member who told them, "Go get your license. I'll use you." The brokerage usually teams the rookie up with an experienced agent, who serves as a mentor, and they share the commission on the transactions that the newbie brings in. This way, everyone at the brokerage wins, and hopefully the newbie doesn't screw up. Usually, after five closings, they'll have earned their wings and won't need supervision anymore. The old days of ruthless managers threatening to fire agents are over. Very few get fired. They just fail out.

As long as rookies are motivated and build their skills, they will make it in this business. It also helps if they get into the business at the right time. Most don't. The best time for an agent to get into the business is when the market is going down, in what we call a buyer's market. Flippers disappear and most agents run for the doors. Learning the business when the market is down or wonky makes for a better agent, because agents typically need to work with buyers before they graduate to listings. It forces them to correctly learn the business, the processes, how to build their business, how pricing works, and how to be of service. What better time to learn than when it's tough?

Conversely, when prices go up, supply goes down, and there are fewer and fewer available customers in an up market. Flippers make money hand over fist, more and more agents flood into the marketplace, and it's easier to sell a home, but there are fewer sales for all the agents. No one really knows when the market has peaked. Soon enough, agents find themselves walking right into a buzz saw. The agent who's been through the tough market will have the moxie for success in any market, so the shock of a market shift won't throttle that agent. This seesaw happens in every single real estate cycle.

If you are still thinking of hiring a rookie, do this exercise: forget that they're in real estate and imagine this person as your doctor, CPA, or attorney. Think about how you'd feel if they said any of this:

- *"I have a ton of time to focus on your needs."*

- *"I'm always available to you night or day."*

> ## SELLER MISTAKE
>
> Hiring someone who isn't highly experienced.

- *"I have the best training, and I am really excited to work with you."*

- *"If there is anything I'm missing, don't worry, I have a mentor."*

- *"If I don't know the answer, then I'll find out for you."*

I don't know about you, but those are some scary words. Run. Away.

SELLER'S AGENT OR BUYER'S AGENT?

Should you hire an agent who mostly represents sellers, represents buyers, or has a good balance of the two? I'm not going to give you the answer; you'll probably figure it out. Yes, some agents are specialists. You've probably picked up that I specialize in representing sellers.

If you need knee surgery, would you go to any orthopedist? Some doctors specialize in knees or shoulders only. This isn't to say that your knee surgery would otherwise be botched but you usually have a choice.

Odds are you will have a more successful knee surgery if your orthopedist specializes in knees.

Real estate is the same. Some agents love working with sellers and choose to specialize in it. All day long they market and negotiate, and put buyers and sellers together. And then they do it over and over again.

A buyer's agent is usually not in the office. They're driving all over the place looking at homes, showing homes, calling agents to see if they have any listings coming up, coordinating inspections, and talking to lenders. An agent that does both really is wearing two very different hats. When selling your house, hire someone who spends most of their time doing just that: selling. If you want to buy a house, then work with an agent who represents a lot of buyers.

> **SELLER MISTAKE**
> Hiring someone who isn't focused on sellers only.

COACHES

Aside from getting help from a manager or a mentor, most agents have worked with a real estate coach. They sign on with coaches for the same reasons professional athletes hire their own personal trainers. Even very experienced top agents have coaches. As a matter of fact, NAR states that "10% of agents complete 90% of all real estate transactions … because they have a coach" (thank you, Pareto principle). Coaches work with an agent's mindset, goals, business planning, and accountability. They push agents and help keep fear from holding them back. I've had a coach for most of my career, and coaching has pushed me to be the best I can be. That gives my clients an advantage. If your agent has a coach, it says a lot.

3

HIRING FRIENDS
AND FAMILY

There is a right and a wrong way to hire your agent. You already know this. There is also the right *person* and the wrong *person* to hire as your next agent.

I'm going to tell you to not to hire a friend or family member to handle your sale. Many sellers have told me they made this mistake. They hire Cousin Margo after hearing she sold grandma's house in two days. Maybe your buddy Steve can sell it. Heck, he has a license. A home sale is often the most complex and important transaction in a lifetime. Shouldn't it be treated as a business decision, and shouldn't you be calling an expert? I know, a friend or family member is always an easy shoulder to tap.

There is a lot on the line when you are selling your home. If you've ever bought or sold a home, you know what an emotional rollercoaster it can be. There were tough decisions, lots of complicated paperwork, unexpected expenses, and lots of second guessing. Even the skilled real estate investor knows that a transaction rarely goes smoothly. So even they try to hire the right person to successfully broker the deal to a close. Over my two decades of selling, I've noticed that the most experienced home sellers tend to treat their sale as a business decision. Many didn't the first few times.

This book is loaded with insights and advice on the type of agent you should hire. If that person just so happens to be a good friend, or a family member, then you are lucky. My mom, dad, and brother were. But I'm willing to bet that you haven't thought this through.

Home sellers who regularly hire friends or family members do so out of guilt, pressure, or entitlement—or maybe they just don't think about it. They get sucked into the "I've-got-to" trap. Imagine if you picked your doctor or lawyer the same way.

Anyone who has bought or sold a home will attest that the success of a sale, as well as the challenges and solutions that arose from the sale, were directly related to the skill level of their agent and their ability to be objective. In real estate, problems can get worse quickly. A skilled agent will have solutions to these problems that you probably didn't even know existed. There are enough challenges without mixing in a close relationship.

In real estate we have a saying: "Bad deals get worse. Good deals don't get better … they just close." Think about that. It's true. I give this advice to new agents all the time. It's a mantra, one of the absolute truths about real estate. Most transactions are tough, and challenges can easily get worse. Yet so many people still risk the ride with a friend or family member.

IF YOU HIRE SOMEONE, DON'T YOU WANT TO BE ABLE TO FIRE THEM TOO?

Everyone knows that a great way to hurt a relationship is to go into business with that person. I don't think that sentence requires any examples to back it up. You're probably already nodding your head. It's tough for a relationship to persevere through what is already a complicated financial process that can be emotional and headache-prone. A real estate sale is always loaded with "if this hadn't happened" or "if that had happened" moments of reflection.

I often find myself competing for listings. It's not uncommon for me to find out that I'm interviewing against one to ten other agents. Often, a friend or family member of the seller is in the mix. In this situation, I'll ask the homeowner to consider the following: do you want to hire someone who you can fire, yell at, and that you don't necessarily need to see at the next family gathering? (Yelling might be the nuclear option, and there's a lot to be said about having that leverage.)

What would be more uncomfortable than seeing a business partner at a family gathering—for the rest of your life? When I bring it up, most of my clients agree that they'd prefer to have a business relationship with their agent. It just makes life easier. If everything goes well, you might have a new friend. If it doesn't, you won't have to see the agent again.

When I get hired in these situations, I offer the seller the perfect script to tell their friend or family member. When they ask, "Why didn't you hire me?" Say this: "I respect and like you too much. I want to keep our relationship intact. I need the ability to yell at you, to question you, and to fire you. Our relationship may not survive a tough situation. I hope you respect my decision to not hire you so that I can have a purely business relationship with someone else."

> **SELLER MISTAKE**
> Hiring a friend or family member under pressure.

SELLING HOMES FOR FAMILY

To be honest, I've handled sales for just about everyone in my family. In these transactions, there was more pressure on me. There was also pressure on them, making every transaction extra tough.

When I sold my mother's home, it was the longest seven months of my life. She had a one-bedroom home in an exclusive Southern California neighborhood called La Canada-Flintridge. It's known for their top ten school district—meaning homeowners pay a premium to live there.

The single-family home was 2,000 square feet, with an upstairs loft and a partially-attached studio guest house. My mother's husband was a successful general contractor and, understandably, they were very proud of what they'd done with the house. So the decision was made to market the home as a three-bedroom. You can probably see where this is going. Yes, it was actually a one-bedroom home. But you do whatever it takes to sell Mom's house, even if it takes 214 days!

In my career of selling over 500 homes, I can count on one hand how many homes (not including condos) that I've sold with only one bedroom.

It was a tough sale already, and every time I called my mother, we had to talk about their home sale. She didn't like it and neither did I. It became the elephant in the room for most of the year. When Christmas came, the home sale was the talk of the family. Who likes to talk about work during the holidays? Not me. I couldn't wait to get that transaction done. Calling my mom in March to let her know that we closed was one of the best phone calls I ever made. It felt good to get my relationship with my mom back to normal. If you're an agent, you know exactly what I mean.

So, when it's time to sell your home, do you ask yourself, "Am I calling a friend or family member, or am I calling an expert?" Thank God it was years ago!

4

HYPING TEAMS, BOUTIQUES, AND ROBOTS

LOOK OUT FOR TEAMS

The average agent handles every aspect of a complex home sale all by themselves. That isn't ideal because no one can be great at everything. It's just easier to break up a transaction into manageable pieces. Most successful agents have help, and others have a lot of help. Some agents have teams. They have multiple agents working on multiple parts of multiple transactions. We've been conditioned to believe that bigger is better, and sometimes these teams are really big. The question is: can "big" be a disservice to the client? The answer is: it depends.

The stand-alone agent does it all. They find buyers and sellers, they preview homes, they place ads in newspapers, create flyers, post homes on the various internet portals, prep the home, stage it, meet photographers and appraisers, schedule showings, handle inspections, deal with all the compliance paperwork, practice psychotherapy here and there … the list is endless. But a lot of this really isn't the job of a successful agent. The problem is that they are busy doing this for multiple clients when they should be focusing on *you*. Do you really want your agent spending their time on most of those administrative tasks, or do you want your agent to be focusing on you? A jack-of-all-trades is a master of none. The fact is, most agents do it all, and some are on a large team.

Teams can be as large as fifty agents, and they like to share everything. They share buyers and sellers, including you and all of the duties necessary to sell your home. NAR's 2021 survey says that a quarter of all agents worked on a team of about four. If you hire a team, you are likely hiring several people without realizing it. It's like asking three linebackers to carry a football for you—it sounds powerful, but how can six hands effectively carry one football? Watch out for the fumbles, and you are definitely going to get passed around.

A team has a lead agent who will be your initial primary contact. This lead agent has a good personality and says all the right things because they have great script practice. They are masters of this domain, and there's a good chance that they will actually show up to a listing or buyer appointment. They will almost always bring along (or send) a "listing coordinator" or "buyer's rep" to the interview. You might not even realize that you are being handed off because you're so sold on the team concept. You will likely be working with no fewer than four different people throughout your transaction. It can be frustrating.

Keep in mind that there are a ton of benefits for the team members. If you're a team member, you can now go on vacation a lot easier than other agents. That agent won't really be missed. Each job has back-ups, and everyone uses checklists and scripts. How would you like your doctor or lawyer to do that to you?

Behind the scenes, teams tend to have a revolving door of members. Someone is always joining, and someone is always leaving. According to NAR's 2021 survey, 47% of agents leave a team within one year. Teams love rookies because they're usually trainable, and the brokerage doesn't have to pay them too much. And rookies love teams because they can learn as much as possible. It's guaranteed income and education before going out on their own. Yes, most members get a small salary with a bonus on closed deals. The problem is that there usually isn't enough business to keep everyone on the team happy with that income, except for the lead agents. What could possibly go wrong?

NOT ALL TEAMS ARE BAD

With small teams there is a premium placed on working with the best people. Sure, I have a small team, but I am extremely involved with my client from beginning to end.

The model and systems I've mastered are fine-tuned. I do the most important tasks, like negotiation and follow-up. I pass the data entry, lockbox installation, paperwork processing, photography, mailers, postcards, and website development off to my licensed assistant. When the reams of disclosure paperwork come in, I review it all, then have my transaction coordinators digitally process and file it for compliance. My clients know that I'm spending my time on *their transaction*, not on someone else's busywork. You want your agent spending their time selling, strategizing and negotiating.

I spend most of my day negotiating, which is what your agent is supposed to be doing. Also, I specialize in seller representation. Over 90% of my business is listings. Helping

SELLER MISTAKE
Working with big teams.

people, interacting with them, negotiating, and selling is what I love to do and I'm able to outsell 99% of the competition. While I also work with my wife, Anne, who is also a Realtor®, my clients never get passed around. Ninety-five percent of the time they hear directly from me. I find this set-up to be perfect for my clients, and I am fortunate that most of my business is repeat and referral business. I certainly *could* sell more homes. But that would require me to pass off important duties to other agents—and we all know what happens when more than one player tries to run the football.

In my opinion, you should hire an agent who has at least one assistant. That way you can have some comfort in knowing your agent is spending their time doing important tasks and they have time for you.

JUST HOW BIG IS YOUR NETWORK?

Every market has small brokerages, often called "boutiques." Many are named after the operating broker. Others have cool names, like my old brokerage, Bradmont Realty. I love small brokerages. Nothing is as inspiring as a start-up company, an entrepreneur, or a company that wants to take on the big brokerages.

You might be surprised to know that according to NAR's 2020 survey, 78% of brokerages had two or fewer agents. When NAR asked what the challenges were with these brokerages, they said it was a lack of listings, exposure, and relevance in the marketplace. They also had difficulty staying current with technology, training, and trends. Hmmm ... at least they admit it.

When I decided to go on my own, I started Bradmont Realty. While I loved taking on the big brands, having a small ten-person brokerage was tough. After many years, I learned that I couldn't compete with the big names that had an insurmountable advantage over what I could offer my clients.

Back then I was a jack-of-all-trades and, unfortunately, a master of none. Representing both sellers and buyers while managing an office and recruiting good agents was incredibly tough. I didn't have a training program, only a mentoring program. I struggled to keep up on the changes and trends in the industry, technology, and legal and liability issues. As a boutique brokerage I wasn't alone in my struggle.

The small brokers in town used to get together to lament how tough the brokerage business was. This was in the 1990s, and there was a lot of brokerage consolidation. After a few meetings, it was clear we had created our own support group. We would help each other and brag about our periodic successes. In the end, I realized that if I wanted to make more money, I would need to be able to provide better and more services to my clients. It was impossible to compete with the offerings of the larger brokerages. When I sold my boutique, I didn't even consider working for a small regional firm.

The small regional firms love to tout their technology and culture. They're like a small internet start-up. They've got the latest gadgets, the coolest sayings, the youngest agents, the hippest office, and the fanciest business cards. Some are actual internet start-ups. Everyone has to tout something when they aren't on a national or international scale. When I had my small brokerage, I had to come up with a lot of BS reasons why my clients should work with me. In real estate, bigger usually is just better.

Most regional firms will talk about their global network, or how they have partnerships, or how they're connected on the web. They use the word "affiliate," which is just a fancy word that doesn't mean that much. It's just a website partnership, or a secondary logo. Big deal. Having a website doesn't make you national or international. It's just a website!

It's just a fact that the larger the brokerage, the more superior the tools, experience, and exposure. An agent is much better equipped with a national or international brand and network. It's a mistake to think otherwise.

The big companies, of course, also have websites. But more importantly, they have boots on the ground. Most big brokerages are national, some are also international. I work at an international brokerage. I've traveled and visited their offices in Canada, Bangkok, the Bahamas, Hong Kong, Costa Rica, and other places throughout the United States. My website shows photos of Anne and our boys standing in front of national and international real estate offices. Every single time I'm back from one of my trips, I wind up either having a client ask for a referral, or I get one. I've met hundreds of agents around the world. We mail notes and Christmas cards to each other. They are real relationships, and it's a real network that I tap into.

Plain and simple, the agent you hire needs to have a huge network, because that is part of the marketplace for your home. The larger the brokerage, the more resources, brainpower, outreach, and liability protection you'll get. The MLS is not enough. You do not know

SELLER MISTAKE

Not seeing the value of a national or international brokerage firm.

where your buyer is going to come from, or how they will find your home. So put the odds in your favor.

TECHNOLOGY—NO SUBSTITUTE FOR AN AGENT

The internet has certainly forced agents to up their games. Until the existence of the internet, the agent was the gatekeeper of information, and everything was in print format. If you wanted to know what was on the market, you went to an agent. If you wanted to know about sales prices, you went to an agent or the county recorder's office, and you looked it up on microfiche.

Now all this information is in the public domain and updated in real time. We all know where to find comparables, listings, walkability scores, crime statistics, trends, permits, school information, and pretty much anything else that will help to make a purchasing decision.

With all this technology, it seems that the transaction should be easier and faster. But it isn't. We thought the same thing when everyone got cell phones. The number one reason sellers use an agent is because they need help with the complexity and the liability of selling a home. According to CAR, the top three seller needs are negotiating price or terms of a sale (59%), determining listing price/strategy (59%), and advice about selling (44%).

Every year, more consumers want to use an agent. This percentage has been increasing, not decreasing. 91% of buyers and sellers used an agent in 2020, up from 69% in 2001. AOL, Yahoo, and eBay all started in 1985. Google started in 1998, and Zillow started in 2006. They've had billions to invest and almost two decades to change what they call an antiquated real estate business model. The fact is that consumers continue to use agents more and more, and recommend them to others. The basic brokerage business model is still doing great.

When the pandemic hit in March of 2020, I found it interesting that almost all technology-based platforms hit the skids because they didn't have their finger on the pulse of the American consumer. Their algorithms and websites were out of whack. Tech didn't know what was really going on and what direction the market was going. They didn't know that there would be a surge in demand for single-family residences. But agents figured it out fast. Clients called their agents and vice-versa. Journalists called agents to find out what was happening. It took technology companies months to catch up.

Many feel that real estate is ripe for disruption. However, a real estate sale is not like renting a movie, catching a ride somewhere, ordering plane tickets, or buying a sweater. Disruption starts with opportunity and the best opportunities arise when there are unhappy customers. Surveys say people are very happy with agents, and they're using them more.

Will technology replace the agent? Not in our lifetime, and here is why.

First off, every home and home sale is unique. Sure, there are condos that can look the same and some tract homes that are indistinguishable. Every home has challenges and benefits. Every transaction consists of a variety of personalities, life and financial goals, liability, timeframes, and more mundane issues such as financing, contingencies, and tax strategy. The human side of each transaction is an integral part of the success. Many in our industry joke that agents act as psychologists throughout a transaction (yes, I've had to talk many clients off the proverbial cliff). Maybe you're watching too many sci-fi movies—I just don't think we'll see technology replacing all these dynamic moving parts in our lifetime.

Secondly, most people don't buy and sell more than three to five times in their lifetimes. The home-buying or selling experience ranks among some of the most important life events, along with getting that first job or getting married. The market is constantly changing, and people need help maneuvering through the process. Also, there are several variables the average person and some agents can't fully see. These include new legislation, legal precedents, financing protocols, current market and design trends, disclosure forms, and even the ever-changing pandemic showing protocols and other challenges that can be difficult to navigate.

The third reason is the complexity of the transaction. Throughout this book, I describe the many moving parts. Even with my experience, I must admit that I am always learning new things: better practices, more efficient strategies, strategic marketing, new laws, and new software and apps. According to CAR, 66% of buyers say it is "very difficult" to buy a home, and 28% of sellers say it is "very difficult" to sell a home.

There is only so much that artificial intelligence can streamline, at least in my lifetime. According to NAR, millennials identified "understanding the home-buying process and steps" as the most difficult item in the home sale journey. They aren't relying on technology to see them through.

The fourth reason is that the size of a real estate transaction is typically the largest of any transaction a person experiences in their lifetime. Real estate transactions keep people awake at night, even when the transaction is going smoothly. There is a huge emotional component to it. Sellers of lower-priced, homogeneous properties will certainly benefit from artificial intelligence. However, as the price increases or market fluctuations happen, more hand-holding is on the menu.

Lastly, there is liability and risk involved, whether you are a buyer or a seller. A real estate transaction is complicated, and the risks and liability constantly change, especially in California. Disclosure laws are always changing and getting more complex. A minor error or omission from a seller can cost tens of thousands in damages. I would love to know what an attorney would think about the prospect of artificial intelligence walking a buyer or seller through a transaction. If something goes wrong, whom do you sue? If you aren't using an agent, then the answer is HAL 9000.

> **SELLER MISTAKE**
> Thinking that technology can replace the human interaction in selling a home.

For the time being, it's safe to say real estate will continue to be a customer service business of humans helping humans. Many real estate pundits write and blog about how agents are being replaced because they believe agents provide fewer services and "don't do anything" to earn their commission. However, the data suggests otherwise. In fact, buyers and sellers are more likely to use the services of a real estate agent the second time they buy or sell a home versus the first time, according to NAR's 2020 survey.

THE iBUYER

An iBuyer is an internet company that buys a home as-is at a reduced sales price for cash, at a future date that the seller chooses. Basically, they are home flippers. It's extremely convenient, but very expensive for the consumer. If you are relocating and you need a guaranteed sale, this might be the way to go. It really is a one-click home sale.

The fact is that the only way the iBuying platform works is if the iBuyer gets a really good deal. What most people don't realize is that the seller actually pays almost double the commission rate of a traditional broker on the sale. The home doesn't go on the market (or the MLS), instead an algorithm determines the purchase price, and that price *needs* to be below market value. The seller gets their home sold on their schedule, as-is, and with no repairs; the iBuyer makes repairs and sells it quickly for what they trust will be a profit.

Most industry veterans see major challenges with the iBuyer model and are skeptical that this model, with such low margins, will ever have a big impact. What's going to happen in a down market when margins are much more at risk? When the market is going up, there is low housing stock coupled with high demand, making iBuying unsustainable because, with tight margins, these companies need to have high volume. More profit from fewer transactions will require them to lower their prices. Why would a seller sell to an iBuyer for a low price when there is high demand? The founder of Opendoor (one of the largest iBuyers) recently commented that their business "is similar to flying a plane, and you have to fix it while you are flying."

Wall Street knows all of this. They love to buy real estate as well, and this is one of their instruments to buy a lot of it because it is so easy for sellers to be taken advantage of (sorry, but this book does prove that point). And the cash needs of these companies are massive and complex: equity investors want massive bets and huge upsides, while debt investors want downside protection. Interestingly, Morgan Stanley, a Wall Street investment banking firm, says the iBuyer platform could get to a 3% market share by 2030.

The internet has changed many businesses and buried others. It has not yet buried the standard real estate brokerage model, and futurists are saying that the agent will not be replaced. However, the transaction will continue to be enhanced with technology. All I'm saying is that there is tremendous value in having a human who uses technology handling your sale.

5

DUAL AGENTS—
A BIG PROBLEM

In real estate, agent representation is serious business. When agents either give advice or represent buyers or sellers, they have created a relationship called *agency.* Agency establishes the most necessary aspect of a transaction: trust.

Dual agency is when the agent who represents the home seller simultaneously represents the home buyer. I'm not going to tell you how big of a mistake this is—yet. That agent is what's called a dual agent. It means the seller's agent and the buyer's agent are the same person, a dual agent. Under dual agency, the agent makes both "ends" of the commission, the seller side, and the buyer side—effectively taking a double commission, otherwise known as "double-ending." Yes, double the commission! As you can imagine, this can be problematic.

Keep in mind that an attorney can only represent one party. There are obvious reasons for this. Why would you want the "other side" to know your bottom line and your motivations? When a transaction is separated between two different agents, then each agent knows only what their prospective client reveals. Dual agency can also occur when there are two different agents in the same brokerage handling your sale.

> **SELLER MISTAKE**
>
> Letting your agent represent you AND the buyer.

How can agents tell the sellers that they're working hard to get the highest price, and then tell the buyers that they're working hard to get them the lowest price?

This is an obvious conflict of interest. Many agents, however, are open to it, or outrightly trying to double-end a deal. It should be obvious that allowing your agent to be a dual agent is a big seller mistake. Rarely are you ever told this.

There are almost two million agents handling five to six million home sales a year. Given the opportunity, most agents would love to double-end a transaction.

THREE TYPES OF AGENCY: BUYER'S, SELLER'S, OR DUAL?

Most consumers don't fully understand real estate agency. This means the implications of the terms also escape them. Let's handle some legal definitions first, courtesy of CAR (the California Association of Realtors®) and the California Civil Code:

> Agency is the relationship or representation created when buyers and sellers seek an agent's advice in a real estate transaction. If there is a licensed agent in the transaction who is not a principal (seller or buyer), then that licensed agent is acting in one of three capacities: the seller's agent, the buyer's agent, or as a dual agent representing both buyer and seller.
>
> A seller's agent, under a listing agreement with the seller, acts as an agent solely for the seller. A seller's agent, or a subagent of that agent, has the following affirmative obligations to the seller: a *fiduciary duty of utmost care, integrity, honesty, and loyalty in dealings with the seller, as well as diligent exercise of reasonable skill and care in the performance of the agent's duties with a duty of honest and fair dealings in good faith, and is not obligated to reveal to either party any confidential information.* They are bound ethically to act in the best interests of their clients. Fiduciary services are the highest degree of services an agent can provide. The buyer's agent owes the same duties to their buyer.

This all might seem straightforward, but there are some interesting facts that most people, even licensed agents, don't know. One is that making a commission has nothing to do with agency or how your agent operates. In other words, even if agents are not earning a commission, they still owe you the above-defined duty of care.

Another thing overlooked is that the California Civil Code advises that all the duties of the dual agent in a real estate transaction do *not* relieve a seller or buyer from their responsibilities to protect his or her own interests. That's right: in dual agency you still need to protect your own interests.

Believe it or not, dual agency is completely legal in most states, including California. In states where dual agency is allowed, the agent can legally represent both the seller and buyer in a transaction—*only with the knowledge and consent of both the seller and buyer.* The dual agent has the same duties as in the paragraphs above: *"A fiduciary duty of utmost care, integrity, honesty, and loyalty. The agent may not, without the express permission of the respective party, disclose to the other party that the seller will accept a price less than the listing price, or that the buyer will pay a price greater than the price offered."*

That's a tough spot for an agent, and for sellers it's tougher if the agent you hired is now representing your buyer, in effect, your opponent.

SELLER MISTAKE
Not understanding your agent's fiduciary duty.

Most state laws require that any agent who has more than a casual relationship with a client needs to present disclosure paperwork explaining agency. NAR says only 27% of agents provide any agency disclosure paperwork at their first meeting with a buyer. NAR doesn't even ask sellers when or whether their agent provided this information.

Agency is so important, however, that the paperwork for disclosing it is always the first set of documents that an agent fills out. However, the paperwork is often buried in the overwhelming stacks of paperwork that many people don't read as carefully as they should.

Additionally, agency disclosure documents are also what lawyers ask for *first* in any real estate dispute.

Another set of facts known in the industry—not by the public—is this: The three issues that cause the most disputes for residential real estate agents are breach of fiduciary duty, misrepresentation, and fair housing. Ask any attorney, brokerage owner, or errors and omissions (E&O) insurance company. They will also tell you that the average dispute costs sellers over $25,000 to resolve. Dual agency is that big of a deal.

DUAL AGENCY CAN NEGATIVELY AFFECT SELLERS

How do sellers assure themselves that they are benefiting from the laws and regulations about dual agency? They can't.

You've probably written offers on a few homes that were rejected. Perhaps you followed up and found out that the listing agent represented the buyer. Maybe that's why you feel you didn't have a chance. It's upsetting. As a buyer, you learned that it's tough to find a great deal, and that the good homes receive a lot of buyer attention. So maybe now you decided to go directly to the seller's agent to increase your chances, knowing that the agent will make a double commission. All you have to do is tell the listing agent that you want to buy the house and you don't have an agent. The buyer is happy, and usually the agent is happy.

But I'm not sure how a seller can be happy when the buyer has an advantage, and their agent makes a double commission. You and your agent need to decide if you will allow this. *Better yet, hope that your agent voluntarily tells you they won't allow dual agency.*

There are a lot of angles to consider. Here's another familiar situation. You've found a home that you want to buy. Your agent calls the seller's agent and asks, "Are you representing a buyer on this transaction?" Depending on state laws, the seller's agent is supposed to answer you with a "yes" or "no". Hopefully, the answer is "no". If the answer is "yes," you need to consider whether you will have a fair chance to buy that home. You also need to ask yourself if the agent is representing other buyers and, if not, then how does the agent choose which buyer to represent, or does the agent represent them all? It's a mess.

"I HAVE MY OWN BUYERS"

When listing agents say they have their own buyers, it takes the wind out of other buyers' sails. Looking at homes and putting together an offer is emotional and time consuming. So, when a buyer finds out the seller's agent has their own buyer(s), they think to themselves, "Why on Earth would anyone want to write an offer with a higher probability of being used or rejected?" After all, if the seller's agent's buyer doesn't get the property, then the agent's paycheck gets cut in half.

There's actually also a chance the seller's agent is going to present your offer to the seller and tell them, "I have a better buyer who will beat this price. I know my buyers, I have a lot of control over them, and you will love this outcome." It usually sounds compelling if the agent knows the script and the seller doesn't know better. Sellers only know what their trusted agents tell them. This is what it's like for other buyers who have no chance: they get used for the advantage of the agent. The other buyers set the price and terms, and then the listing agent swoops in with their own buyer—and a double commission.

As you can see, dual agency discourages buyers and the market. When it is abused, it causes sellers to get fewer offers and they probably end up with a lower sales price. Is this provable? In court, many times it is—even out of court. Overall, it's common sense.

Only a few seller's agents will say something to a potential buyer to the effect of, "I won't represent a buyer on this transaction, so I encourage you to write an offer." A statement like that is like hearing "Bingo!" You now have a fair opportunity to write an offer that will be objectively presented to the seller, knowing that you won't be competing with the seller's agent. *Giving the marketplace a fair chance is exactly how to get to market price!*

It's no surprise that many buyers feel that they need to go to the listing agent to buy a house. Some have told me they always do that. I don't blame them. Still, everybody gets used, especially the other bidders and the seller. This happens so often and, to be honest, I'm tired of it.

If your agent is a dual agent, you might want to ask how the brokerage handles multiple offers when one of the buyers is also represented by your agent. In most brokerages, the assistant manager or manager might step in only during the bidding process to help provide a level playing field. *Even if a manager steps in during negotiations, the agent is still making double the commission, still represents both sides, and other buyers know they are competing with the seller's agent, which can disenfranchise potential buyers.* After, the dual agent usually handles everything from there, including negotiations for concessions.

Again, how do dual agents push hard for a buyer concession when they are also representing the seller? Let's take it a step further. How much more difficult is it for the dual agent to treat each side fairly when the agent has a much longer or deeper relationship with the seller? Maybe your agent has a much longer and deeper relationship with the buyer than with you.

WHY DOES DUAL AGENCY STILL EXIST?

Dual agency in residential real estate is still popular, yet NAR doesn't provide any statistics on how often it occurs. However, a search of nationwide MLS listings suggests anywhere from 10% to 20% of all deals are dual agency transactions. Keep in mind that intended dual agency transactions don't always work out. Some transactions don't make it all the way to a closing (and for good reason), so the above estimate is low.

Often, a seller thinks that having the same agent handle both sides of the transaction is a *plus*—especially if the agent convinces the seller that this is beneficial to them. It sounds efficient and easy, and most agents will tell you with a smile that it is no big deal.

> **SELLER MISTAKE**
>
> Not asking their agent enough of the right questions.

Of course, many of my colleagues love real estate for the opportunity to "double pop" the commission. It's easy because buyers often call the listing agent directly, and agents know this. This is why we have a saying in real estate: "The listing agent is king." Listing agents have a huge amount of power in real estate transactions because they control all access to the property and the seller. And even though my colleagues won't enjoy reading this, we've all noted to each other that "having a real estate license is like having a license to steal." *Sellers and buyers are just too easy to take advantage of because they trust their agents implicitly and don't ask the right questions at the right time.*

According to NAR surveys, the top three factors that consumers consider when choosing a real estate agent are reputation, honesty, and trustworthiness. Dual agency tends to both destroy reputations and give clients an opening to question an agent's trustworthiness. It tends to be fueled by greed, creating problems for both consumers and brokerages alike.

Despite legislative efforts by Realtor® associations in states across the country, dual agency is still allowed in most states, including California where state lawmakers have lowered the standards of representation; it just needs to be disclosed. However, Alaska, Colorado, Florida, Kansas, Maryland, Oklahoma, Texas, Vermont, and Wyoming either ban the practice of dual agency or severely limit it to a functionary (or transactional) agency, in which an agent works with both the buyer and seller but has *no fiduciary responsibility* to either party. A fiduciary can easily do functionary work; a functionary cannot easily do fiduciary work. These states that ban or limit it have not relaxed their laws. It's that important to them.

The Consumer Federation of America, an association of 300 nonprofits totaling fifty million members, has been calling for states to ban dual agency and make disclosures less confusing. "Buyers and sellers often don't understand the role their broker plays," the group reported. "Today, many home buyers and sellers do not know whether their agent is representing their interests, those of the other party, or those of neither," said Stephen Brobeck, a CFA senior fellow.

MORE DOWNSIDES OF DUAL AGENCY

NAR tracks legal trends and surveys agents on the types of legal issues they encounter through an online system called Legal Scan. Incredibly, every year, over a third of all survey respondents reported a "moderate or high level of current disputes involving agency issues." A quarter of all respondents said that they believed there was a significant need for training on agency issues in general. Numerous surveys bear this out. The fact is that agents usually gloss over agency concerns. If you've interviewed an agent, you know how easy it is to focus on strategy, staging, or marketing instead of something as dry as agency. And why would some agents want to cut out their opportunity to double their pay?

Recently, the State of New York Office of General Counsel published a memo titled, "Be Wary of Dual Agency." The office cautioned consumers that "by consenting to a dual agency you are giving up your right to have your agent be loyal to you since your agent is now also representing your adversary. Once you give up that duty of loyalty, the agent can advance interests adverse to yours. For example, once you agree to dual agency, you may need to be careful about what you say to your agent. Although your agent still cannot breach any confidences, your agent may not use the information you give him or her in a way that advances your interests."

Earning a double commission is extremely tempting for most agents. As you've probably figured out by now, one reason homes don't sell is that the seller's agent is favoring their own buyer(s) and try to double-end one of their own clients. Sellers are often unaware of these shenanigans. I've been hired too many times as the second or third agent to sell a home that ended up selling easily just because we welcomed all buyers. It wasn't rocket science.

AVOIDING A LAWSUIT

Dual agency is also an easy way to get into a lawsuit. It may be unfair, but dual agency provides easy targets for attorneys because dual agents have trouble proving that they didn't stifle competition, that they represented their client, and got the highest price for a seller. If you ask for legal advice prior to hiring an agent, you will definitely be told to not allow dual agency. I work with a lot of attorneys, and I can't tell you how many of them tell me, "Had they just asked me before selling their house, they wouldn't be in this predicament." Some agents will flat out tell buyers that they have no other options to get the house. If these agents don't flat out demand buyers' business, then they will give hints to that effect. See the chapter about open houses for other instances of what many attorneys deem more predatory behavior from agents.

If your agent doesn't voluntarily explain agency, then you either need to let them know how important it is to you or move on to a different agent. It needs to be discussed.

WHAT DO LEADERS SAY?

As much of a problem as it is in California, our legislature has rarely made a successful push to limit or outlaw dual agency. CAR spearheads the arguments to keep dual agency legal. Yes, you read that correctly. They make two arguments: first, that it's unfair that a potential buyer can't go directly to the seller's listing agent if they want to buy their home. Second, the buyer shouldn't be forced to represent themselves or find a blank offer form on their own. I guess that our legislators fear that a buyer might not be able to find an agent. Remember there are over two million licensed agents.

The commercial brokerage industry also supports dual agency. Represented by the American Industrial Real Estate Association (AIR), they feel that doing away with dual agency would harm small businesses by adding costs and affecting relationships. They reason that consumers should be able to go straight to the listing agent if they have a pre-existing relationship, such as from a tenant lease extension. They also feel that doing away with dual agency would eliminate freedom of choice, as it would provide certain firms with additional commission fees for services that are not wanted, but rather, are mandated by law.

NAR and CAR want to preserve dual agency; it says so right on their websites. They even fundraise and have an action fund for it. If you search "Fighting for Our Profession" under CAR or NAR, you will find that the top two priorities of both NAR and CAR are preserving dual agency and the mortgage interest deduction. Go ahead and Google it.

NAR has money, connections, influence, and resources that are usually put to very good use. Keep in mind, as with many large organizations, not all members agree with every effort. You may have noticed that I am an

NAR member. That's because I'm with a national brokerage, and since they are members of NAR, I am therefore required to pay my NAR dues. You could say that I'm forced into it.

WHEN I QUIT DUAL AGENCY

Over the course of several years, I sold three houses for Dave, one of my best friends from high school. One of these sales was of his luxury townhome in South Pasadena back in 2010. After three months of relative inactivity, an interested couple called me from Florida. They said they didn't know a single person in California, so I asked Dave for his permission to represent them. Dave agreed, and those Floridians flew out and bought the home. Dave was thrilled with the sale, and I felt I had been extremely fair to both sides. Later that year, however, Dave made an offhand remark about how much money I made double ending the sale. This was my best friend saying this, not a normal client. I'm a sensitive guy, so it bothered me. I felt like I did something wrong, and it made a lasting impact on my career. That's when I stopped being a dual agent. Thank you, Dave.

In the long run, dual agency wasn't good for my business. I built my career on referral and repeat business. I rarely advertise. I work hard to make my clients happy with my service and ask them for referrals, as any good salesman should. I also track where my business comes from. I always felt I represented my clients at a high level, but on transactions where I was the dual agent, I received fewer referrals. When I stopped, it was a shock to my old manager. Nevertheless, he also said he respected my decision.

The importance of preserving a good reputation was another reason not to represent buyers on my seller transactions. Agents know the local agents who practice dual agency. These agents aren't overly respected. Other agents try to avoid the big abusers because we all know our buyer will be competing with their buyer(s). Imagine being an unsuspecting seller who hires one of these agents. While buyers and sellers don't know who they are, the agents do. They think their agent is the hardest working agent in the area! They *seem* to bring more buyers than the other agents.

No one will tell you what their reputation is. Most sellers never find out because critiquing another agent to a member of the public has major legal ramifications. If I told you who the dual agency abusers were, I'd probably get sued!

SINGLE AGENCY: GREAT FOR BUSINESS

Not representing two sides of a deal has several benefits. Local agents know their buyers have as fair a chance as anyone at my listings. They look at my properties very differently and want to show them. Lazy agents will tell their buyers to call me for information, knowing I won't steal their clients. This leads to my listings getting more offers than most other homes and generating bidding wars as well.

Saying no to dual agency means I get hired more often, and I get more referrals. When I have the chance to explain to home sellers how I'll be their advocate from beginning to end, I almost always get hired. *In many cases, the seller says I'm the only agent who offers single-party seller representation, a high-level fiduciary service.*

I am often asked what I do when a buyer calls me and says they don't have an agent and they want to work with me to get a home that I have listed. I tell the buyer that I have an agreement with the seller that specifies I cannot represent a buyer on this transaction, though I am happy to tell them everything about a property. Prospective buyers almost always thank me, often admitting that they already have an agent and will stick with that person. These buyers lose what they hoped would be an inside track, but I tell them I don't play that way and that everyone has the same fair chance to buy the home.

> **SELLER MISTAKE**
> Not finding out from the start whether your agent is a Dual Agent.

Rarely does that conversation end poorly. I even offer to help buyers find an agent to work with if they really do not have an agent. Yes, I'll find them an agent! There are approximately two million real estate agents in the U.S. That means one in every 152 Americans has a real estate license. In California that ratio is closer to one in 40. The funny thing is, rarely does anyone need the referral.

FIND YOUR TRUE ADVOCATE

The dual agency conversation should be a significant talking point, and it should happen early in the interview process. When interviewing agents to sell your home, keep note of those who tell you upfront and voluntarily that they will be your advocate from start to finish. These agents get bonus points. If you interview enough experienced agents in your area, you will find someone who values the importance of this devoted relationship and high-level fiduciary service. If that happens, take a moment to smile.

Once you've found your top agent and avoided dual agency, are you all set? Not yet. You're still far from the finish line; there are many more mistakes you'll need to avoid during the sale of your home.

6

GOING IT ALONE

One of the worst things you can do as a homeowner is to try to sell your home on your own. Everyone thinks about it. In the industry, we call this a FSBO (For Sale by Owner, pronounced "fizz-bow"). FSBO sellers want to save on the commission. Also, some don't like agents, and I know how that feels. I have to work with annoying agents every single day!

Successfully going it alone is difficult and unlikely. I hate to break the bad news, but 92% of all FSBO sellers eventually list with a licensed agent, according to NAR. That's right. Nine out of ten give up.

As I mentioned earlier in the book, what might also be surprising is that working with an agent is becoming more and more prevalent. Again, NAR said 69% of all home sellers used an agent in 2001, back when Google was just a few years old. By 2019 it was at 89%, and by 2020 that percentage increased to 91%. FSBO sales have remained near the lowest levels recorded by NAR, at 6% of all sales. The other sales without agents were mostly homes purchased directly from a builder, inter-family sales, or foreclosures.

SELL YOUR HOME BY YOURSELF, NET LESS MONEY

Clearly, FSBOs don't feel an agent's services are worth a commission. However, there have been multiple studies showing that FSBO sellers don't actually save any money. Conduct your own research and you'll find the same conclusion. However, be careful not to get biased opinions from services that dislike agents or from companies that sell discounted services to FSBO sellers. Be sure to steer clear of websites that claim to help you with open houses. They all target FSBO sellers, saying things like "Buy our signs and put your home up on our website. We've helped hundreds just like you. Follow our plan and save lots of money!" (Check out Chapters 9 and 10!)

The real data shows that when FSBOs do work, they actually tend to sell for lower prices than comparable home sales. And, in many cases, they net a sale below the average differential represented by the prevailing commission rate. If the differential was significant, then wouldn't FSBO-ing be more popular? The fact is, saving money on the front end causes a FSBO seller to lose money on the back end—for many reasons.

FSBOs attract buyers who rationalize lower bids with the logic that the seller is saving traditional commission. Such buyers might search for and target sellers who are not being represented by agents. In other words, *bargain hunters shop FSBOs more often.* I hate to say this, but most buyers look at the FSBO seller as an amateur—and aren't they? FSBOs are rarely more experienced than even the most rookie of agents. At least rookie agents have learned the basics: they have the MLS, training, a network, and the right forms. It just rarely works out for the FSBO seller.

A great example comes from *The Wall Street Journal*, which reported that the founder of forsalebyowner.com, Colby Sambrotto, spent six months trying to sell his New York City condominium by himself. He was trying to sell his 2,000-square-foot apartment using online listings and classified ads. He eventually turned over the listing, with full commission, to a broker. Believe it or not, the broker concluded that the condo was

SELLER MISTAKE

Thinking you will make more money by selling your home yourself.

priced too low. The agent listed it in the MLS, and it went under contract after attracting multiple offers. The condo closed for $150,000 more than the asking price Sambrotto had originally set. Go ahead and Google Sambrotto's story.

THE MLS—HERE TO STAY

Consumers want and need access to as much information as possible, and sellers want exposure to the largest audience. The MLS provides this.

The MLS is where 89% of all homes get sold, according to NAR. Throughout the United States, there are over 800 of them that function as portals for licensed agents to share listing data. These lists of homes share a common network, so a listing on one MLS is almost always on all the others. The system facilitates cooperation among competitors, allowing the buyer to access more listings and the seller to access more buyers. Agents on the MLS agree to compensate each other if they sell each other's listings, incentivizing the agents to show and sell the property and enlarging the buyer pool. In addition, properties listed with an MLS-affiliated broker are also listed online with other participating broker websites, thus marketing the home to a huge buyer population. The more buyers who see the home … well, you know the rest.

With rules and standards for accurate information, everyone is on a level playing field with the MLS. Realtors® also want and need a reliable source of information so they can do their job effectively. Because they know the MLS is policed heavily, appraisers and lenders can rely on the MLS information for what they do. There are several requirements that MLS members must follow, and inaccurate data gets flagged with a violation. If it is not corrected, it can progress to fines, and can eventually lead to an agent being kicked off the platform. Could you imagine if this was open to the public? It would be impossible to ensure the integrity of the data.

Many don't realize that the MLS is not a platform to market the agent or the brokerage. It's a platform to market properties. The agent cannot advertise on the platform. Agents' information or even a photo of their real estate sign isn't allowed in the public-facing marketing comments and photos. The MLS doesn't have sponsors, ads, or any way to give more exposure to one property over others. If you were a buyer's agent, you probably wouldn't want your buyers directly marketed to by listing agents. As a seller, you do want buyers to have access to your listing with no less exposure than the other listings. As you can see, the MLS is intended to be cooperative.

THE MENTAL STRAIN OF A FSBO

Aside from losing money, I think the worst part of being a FSBO is losing your mind in the process. The reason? FSBO sellers quickly realize that selling a house is extremely stressful. According to the Harris Poll, in 2018, 80% of consumers said that buying or selling a home is "a stressful process"—even with a professional agent! Consider the disadvantages:

- Not being able to market on the most powerful platforms
- Not having the right forms
- Not knowing how to price a home
- Not knowing disclosure and contract laws
- Not having access to or knowledge of the local market
- Not having any experience negotiating with other agents
- Not incentivizing agents to show your house

To add to the stress are the unrelenting phone calls from agents. Agents love to call FSBOs. They're all hoping to call when the FSBO has given up. Ninety percent of them do just that. These sellers are great leads!

After all, the FSBO seller has already given their name, phone number, address, and email to the world. Most agents employ enticing scripts to encourage the seller to give up. Others are used to figure out how frustrated you are so they can find your breaking point. After all, these agents are trained killers—I mean, professionals.

If possible, it gets even more aggravating. Some of these agents will call and say they have a buyer, just so they can start a conversation. News flash: most don't. They just want to keep you on the phone to dig for more information and see if you're ready to call it quits.

Assuming the FSBO owner offers a buyer's commission, the seller will still be in a tough situation. The seller won't typically have the most up-to-date contract and disclosure forms nor the vendor contacts for the title, escrow, termite inspection, home warranty, etc. These sellers tend to think they can rely on the escrow company (sorry, no), the closing attorney (maybe), or the buyer's agent for these documents. And to make it more difficult, these vendors don't really like working with FSBOs. These sales are more work for them; they fall apart more often, and the sellers require a ton of hand-holding. Even though FSBO sellers are more work, it is against the law for these vendors to charge them more.

The FSBO sellers could also cut a deal with a buyer's agent to represent both sides of the transaction to provide all the necessary paperwork and liability protection, and now they would be in a dual agency situation. Do you really think the buyer's agent is on your side? (See Chapter 5). FSBOs really are going at this alone.

> **SELLER MISTAKE**
>
> Not realizing the amount of work and stress involved as a FSBO.

WON'T AN ESCROW COMPANY HANDLE A LOT OF THE FORMS FOR A FSBO?

Many FSBO sellers believe they can just have their escrow company process all the paperwork. The challenge many face, at least in California, is that escrow companies are highly regulated and are required to conduct their business within the boundaries of their stated business mission. After all, escrow is supposed to be a neutral third party that handles the sale at the direction of both the buyer and the seller. They do not represent buyers or sellers and provide no advisory function. They have escrow licenses, not real estate brokerage licenses, and their liability carriers won't allow them to function as an agent or to provide sales contracts, disclosures, or advice. Too often, the FSBO seller realizes this only after the sale has been negotiated, putting them in a tough and vulnerable spot.

Some FSBO sellers wind up hiring a real estate attorney. You should know that their fees can cost as much or more than a commission. At that point, unforeseen problems usually pop up that can be cumbersome and require concessions since you might be providing late disclosures such as a faulty repair, recurring maintenance issues, unpermitted work, insurance claims, or even a leaky pool. They might also use the wrong forms and wording.

Some attorneys decide to write their own disclosure packages. In this case, the client will want to make sure that they are getting covered appropriately. Every state has an association of Realtors® that provides their members with a wide variety of forms. However, they don't provide them to FSBOs or anyone who isn't a member. Which forms to use can be confusing. Each transaction requires about twenty to thirty different forms, and there is *no such thing as a standard package of forms.* Most transactions are unique, some require certain forms, and using the wrong forms could easily increase your liability as a FSBO. Some transactions allow for fewer disclosure forms, and accidentally using too many unnecessary ones might seem like a good idea. The problem is that the sloppier the transaction, the more liability you create for yourself. My forms library holds over 300 different forms, and even though I sell a lot, I still need to use a checklist and have my assistant double-check everything. It's complicated.

SELLER MISTAKE

Not being aware of the liabilities and legalities as a FSBO.

If you are going to hijack these forms, then you should know that each form states that they cannot be copied without permission. If that permission isn't granted, there might be even more problems for the FSBO seller. There are always updates to the countless forms, not to mention new forms are added all the time. When the pandemic hit, almost a dozen new forms were added to our catalog, six in one week alone! The paperwork and the requirements are constantly changing and growing. As an agent, I am amazed at anyone who would try this alone.

Another issue is that a FSBO seller doesn't have E&O insurance—something that many, but not all agents have. If you, as a FSBO seller, make an error, or forget to disclose something, then you've potentially exposed yourself to a liability nightmare. If the buyer is represented by an agent, then they have this coverage. And yet, it doesn't cover you. I'm not aware of coverages less than $500,000, and most brokerages in my area have coverages of at least $10 million.

Attorneys know that a FSBO seller doesn't have what a real estate brokerage has in their back pocket: transaction coordinators, office managers, in-house attorneys who deal with these issues all the time, and the ultimate fail-safe: skilled E&O insurance attorneys. FSBO sellers just don't have that backup.

Going it alone will definitely create liability and headaches. Once you close you may not sleep well for years. Or at least until the statute of limitations runs its course. You just hope that you handled everything correctly.

PAPERWORK AND LIABILITY PROTECTION

How does a FSBO seller protect themselves without an agent representing them? Most don't know they need liability protection and know nothing about disclosure laws. I'm not aware of any state that allows a seller to avoid disclosing known defects. The most common lawsuit against a FSBO seller is failure to disclose.

Many FSBO sellers believe they need to specify they are selling "as-is" and they have liability coverage. *Selling as-is does not absolve the seller from disclosing what they are required to disclose.* Yes, you must disclose what you're aware of, with other caveats. For example, in California our Civil Code § 2079 states that a seller is "… to disclose to that prospective buyer all facts materially affecting the value or desirability of the property." There are many other requirements in the statute as well. Deaths, nuisances, insurance claims, and other disclosures are statutory (required under state law), even in an as-is sale.

BUT AGENTS FSBO THEIR OWN HOMES, RIGHT?

Rarely.

I've bought and sold my own homes more than thirty times in my life. Other than the few times I've bought directly to get a great deal, I always hired agents. Yes, I'm a broker and I've paid hundreds of thousands in commissions. Like everyone else, I don't want to pay commissions. But the fact is that real estate doesn't sell itself. Knowledgeable salespeople are necessary to help the process along and, most of the time, those commission dollars were very well spent.

Right now, I'm flipping a property. I bought a home in Pasadena that needs everything: a new bathroom, kitchen, drains to the street, a roof, central air and heat, electrical panel, and plumbing throughout. On top of that, it needs all new doors, landscaping, the floors redone, and the usual little things, plus paint and hardware. I'm spending six figures to fix it, and I will still get a very good return for my work and risk. Yet even with my long years of professional experience buying and selling, I will have an agent list the home. Sellers, even top agents like me, have blind spots, and need advice. My agent Tara has helped me determine the best strategies for selling so the house gets top dollar. And I'm paying a full commission!

If, after hearing all this about FSBO, you still want to go it alone, then at least stage your home. FSBO sellers routinely skip this important step because they don't have a professional explain it to them or help them prep the home. The "HGTV Effect" is real; buyer expectations are high, especially if they're millennials. Preparing your home for sale is different than living in it. It needs to appeal to the widest range of potential buyers, most of whom do not share your personal style. Buyers struggle to envision themselves in a home if the one they're looking at doesn't immediately suit their tastes.

Don't sell your home alone. The process can take longer and cost you more money and grief than you might ever imagine.

■ ■ ■

A LOOK AT BUYER PROFILES

After being in the real estate industry for many years, agents come to recognize that many buyers will fall into categories. The following profiles are not just for FSBOs to consider, as anyone involved in real estate should keep an eye out for them; however, it is in a FSBO's best interest to understand these buyers and how best to approach each type. The following buyer profiles are well-known in the industry, and account for a large portion of those you'll meet.

The Liars

Anyone in the real estate business has heard the saying "buyers are liars" many times. It's mean. Is it true? Some buyers *will* say anything to get into a transaction. Some promise to hire you but made that promise to other agents as well. Some say they are qualified for loans—they aren't. Some say they're easy to work with—and then they turn into nightmares. Every single experienced agent has muttered "buyers are liars" at least once. FSBOs have to deal with them as well. There's no way to avoid them. Still, knowing they're out there might help.

The Looky-Loo

Lots of Looky-Loos roam through open houses on Sunday afternoons. These include the swarms of neighbors and folks driving around doing errands and impulsively stopping off to see your house. Sometimes, a few real buyers join in the mix. They usually don't have an agent and haven't gone through the pre-approval process. "We're just looking" is their moniker. As important as digital marketing is, it's still a numbers game: most online clicks are from looky-loos as well. FSBOs might try to follow up with them. I assure you, it's a waste of time.

The All-Cash Bully

Because financing isn't an issue, the family with a suitcase full of cash can understandably look strong. They can close quickly and get everyone to the finish line. Sometimes these buyers are your best bet. However, this bully frequently expects a discount and quick response times. In a cash barter, the buyer's agent will be bullish, reminding the listing agent that they're on the cusp of an easy and fast close.

If the house is in good enough condition to get a bank loan, then the seller might be able to get more money with a loan-contingent buyer. However, this could extend the process by weeks. Consider that you can always use the cash offer as leverage to get the loan-contingent buyers to the best price and terms that a cash buyer won't go to.

The Sympathy Seekers

These buyers submit their offer with a "love letter" explaining who they are and why they love the house, in the hope of fostering a connection that might get them the deal or a discount. They'll write about how long they've been searching, and usually they will tip their hand as to how motivated they are to buy. While these love letters can be genuine, you shouldn't rely on them too much. Try to avoid buyer photos or other personal information that can lead to discriminatory accusations.

The Scrappy Dark Horse

Most buyers fall into this category: they work two jobs, have kids, debt, not a huge bank balance, and might even need parent money to make the transaction happen. The lender can ask to extend their loan and appraisal contingency time periods as well. Home inspections don't always get done quickly, nor does the appraisal. A FSBO seller will get antsy with this buyer, as they contrast dramatically with the all-cash folks. However, dark horses will close the deal because they need to.

The Snake in the Grass

The snake in the grass is hard to spot; some are impossible to identify until it is too late. The offer comes in, all nice and smooth with a great price, terms, and maybe even short contingency periods. On paper, they look like a winner. However, once this buyer's offer is accepted, sellers find themselves on a rollercoaster ride—and sometimes it's the ride from hell. This buyer might abuse the provisions of the contract, wait until the last minute to complete a wide range of investigations and contingency removals, and string the seller along to negotiate concessions, whether for repairs, credits, or price reductions. All too often the buyer's agent is in cahoots with these snakes.

Snake-in-the-grass types are much more harmful when a home has been on the market for some time, because they know they are the only game in town with no backup buyer for the seller to use as leverage. Snakes can really create havoc for the seller. When these buyers give their reports to the seller's side (either to the seller or seller's agent), the seller is now aware of the report's findings, which means if the snake backs out of the transaction, the seller has a responsibility to provide all these reports as disclosures to the new buyers. The seller is now backed into a corner and forced to negotiate the price down.

It gets even worse if your sale falls apart. The new buyers will often want their own expert to review the reports, because most of these experts will not be willing to give their opinions unless they can do their own inspections. Imagine every single report being reviewed by a new inspector. The inspector will no doubt want to impress the buyer by finding even more issues with the house. What a nightmare.

> **SELLER MISTAKE**
> Not knowing the types of buyers you will run into when you sell your home yourself.

Just hire a professional.

7

NOT NEGOTIATING

I hope that you're convinced by now that you shouldn't try to sell your home yourself. In this chapter, I also hope to convince you that your agent needs to be a great negotiator. Whatever your preconceived notions are about agents, please don't assume they're all good negotiators. The best way to figure out if you're hiring the right negotiator is to negotiate fees and terms with your prospective listing agent. The best salespeople are the best negotiators, they're the most successful in this business, and they will probably net you the most money.

Typically, the seller hires a seller's (listing) agent, and that agent splits that commission between the seller's office and the buyer's agent's brokerage, usually by offering a cooperating buyer's commission on the MLS.

Commission rates vary among different regions and circumstances. They are not set by law, and they are negotiable. Due to United States antitrust laws, I unfortunately cannot give you real-world numbers. I wouldn't want anyone to think that I was price-fixing or trying to influence the marketplace.

Often, sellers base their hiring decision on how low of a commission they can negotiate. It stands to reason that this is a great way to save money. I would argue that if that's how you make your decision on an agent, that there's a very good chance you're about to lose thousands or tens of thousands of dollars—or even more. I say this because you probably didn't hire a good negotiator. I'm sure it feels good to push around your agent. But, if you can push your agent around, then so can everyone else. Hopefully your agent is going to be a better negotiator than you, right?

The best way to figure out if you're hiring the right negotiator is to negotiate *with them*. The quality of the words that come out of your agent's mouth is in direct proportion to their success—and to yours.

> ## SELLER MISTAKE
> ### Being able to out-negotiate your own agent.

If you are like most sellers, you want to walk away with the most money possible. As you go through the interview process, I want you to keep something in mind. You are probably thinking that if you can find an agent who is willing to work for less, that would be a good thing. When an agent tells you what their fee is, they're telling you something very important about themselves. They're telling you what kind of negotiator they are. You have to decide whether you want a strong negotiator representing you, a safe negotiator representing you, or a weak negotiator representing you.

The higher the fee, the higher the chance is that you've found a skilled negotiator. If they're charging a slight discount, then that's someone who plays it safe, and they're going to give your money away in the end. If they give you a big discount, then you are dealing with someone very new or very weak, and that agent likely gives even more money away to get a deal done.

How can you expect someone to stand up for you and fight for every last dollar when they can't stand up for themselves?

The fact is, negotiating a commission will usually net you more money than getting a discount broker to handle your sale, as long as you don't make other typical seller mistakes.

DISCOUNT BROKERAGES

Do you shop for a surgeon, a lawyer, a general contractor, or your kid's tutor primarily on price? Would it bother you if the first thing they said, without even asking, was "I'm going to give you a discount?" Do successful people really need to offer discounts? If they do, then don't they have to "make it up with volume?" That's appealing to an agent. But, if they get a lot of repeat business (assuming it's for providing great service and getting great results) would they still need to offer discounts? If the discount brokerage model works, wouldn't the majority of sellers use them? Wouldn't commission rates be going down substantially? The fact is that they aren't, and discount brokers don't get much repeat business. Even in real estate, you get what you pay for. It's my opinion that most people hire discount brokers because they think it doesn't matter who you hire, the result will be the same. If that's the way you feel at this point in reading, please email me at mike@michaelbbell.com for a full refund on this book.

If you've tried to sell your home using a discount brokerage, did you notice how badly they want to do open houses? That's because discount brokers need to maximize their efforts. All of them (yes, all of them) use open houses for three reasons. First, it sounds great when they tell you that they will do open houses until it sells. Second, the discount brokerage model isn't geared toward service by taking care of showings at a moment's notice. A discount broker will rarely offer to take a buyer through alone. They will suggest viewing the home at the upcoming open house. "Push them to the open house" is their industry jargon. Finally, it's an opportunity for the discount brokers to snag buyers to double-end a sale to make up for the discounted commission. Chapter 9 is all about open houses so keep reading.

For some sellers, the primary reason for hiring an agent is the discounted commission. I'm not saying you can't save some cash during a home sale. However, all too often, saving money on the front side means losing money at the end. You can always find a discount broker for anything; these agents are everywhere. So are discounted lawyers, doctors, tax preparers, eye doctors, and pharmacists. Is real estate service really something to skimp on? Discount brokerages that offer low commission rates in large letters in their online ads can seem appealing, and they have a ton of Wall Street money behind them. The logic behind moving to online discount brokerages was to grab a massive listing market share and use that as leverage to generate a much larger pool of buyers for their agents. Even small boutique offices will list high-end properties at ridiculously low commission rates just so they can use them for self-promotion. These are called their "loss leaders," and most small companies need to do this to compete. You might think that these brokers are the way to go. However, they haven't proven to be big disruptors in the industry. Why not? Why do so many of them fold? Why don't they get a lot of repeat and referral business? If they did, then there would be a tectonic shift in the industry, and we haven't seen it. The fact is, internet brokerages do not handle the majority of home sales in the United States.

The largest discount brokerage company happens to be publicly traded, and they don't even have salespeople on commission. Their agents are employees. I don't have anything against having a job. The fact is, if you can't make it as an agent in sales, then you get a salaried, usually lower-paying, job. It's harsh but true. Do you want a successful salesperson—a *real* real estate agent—negotiating for you, or someone who didn't make it in sales?

If you've ever hired a discount broker, then you've probably experienced a level of service that didn't thrill you. Your agent is likely on a team. When you call the firm, it's likely that you will be talking to a salaried team member, and if the person on the phone can't handle the conversation, then you get transferred to someone else. Guess what? An inquiring buyer for your home or buyer's agent will experience the same frustration.

Commissions can be challenging to negotiate, and to an inexperienced seller, commissions seem like lots of money. If you search hard, you might find someone willing to represent you for a few hundred dollars. But beware: you get what you pay for. Larger, more established brokerages have a large array of marketing services they provide. If these services are not interesting to you (for whatever reason), then you may want to work with smaller brokerages that will provide fewer services and lots of open houses. They have fewer expenses, provide less marketing reach, and they tend to discount their commissions.

So why have average real estate commissions in the United States barely decreased since the online brokers busted into the industry in the 1990s? And with all the technological advances available, why have an agent and pay a commission at all?

Over the last two real estate cycles (basically, when the market goes up then back down), commission rates went slightly down as values went up, because there were more agents flooding into the market and they undercut themselves. The flip side is true. An example was during the great recession after 2007, when Fannie Mae and Freddie Mac actually stipulated that higher commissions be paid to agents. Banks were trying to cut commissions on their short sales and foreclosures. Even the government realized that sellers "get what they pay for."

> **SELLER MISTAKE**
> Thinking that saving money on commissions will net you more money in the end.

NEGOTIATE THE COMMISSION WITH YOUR AGENT

A *Consumer Reports* survey of thousands of readers who sold a property found that among the 46% of sellers who asked for a reduction in the agent's commission, 71% were successful. How much respect did those agents lose at that point? A third of all agents were out-negotiated by their clients! Once offers come in, how do you think the negotiations on price and other concessions were handled? Hello.

According to NAR's 2021 Home Buyer and Seller Generational Trends survey, 44% of real estate agents initiated the discussion of commission. What? Shouldn't the seller initiate that discussion? Who is supposed to be the professional negotiator? How would you feel if your agent negotiated the price of your home before the buyer asked if it was negotiable? Well, that might be happening 44% of the time!

Keep your eyes and your ears open during the commission negotiation process. This is the moment when you'll know whether the agent sitting in front of you is good or great. If the agent is a weak negotiator, you will be able to negotiate their fee down. That agent will probably not negotiate your home sale much better. You could just hope that agent negotiates better for you when it really matters. Or, if the interview reveals an agent's inability to negotiate, you might consider hiring a someone else. By the way, picking an agent because they will pay for staging is not a good idea either.

■ ■ ■

HIGH-END HOME SELLING

In every luxury marketplace there are usually a handful of agents who dominate. Reducing their commission is rarely the reason why these agents succeed, however. No, they dominate because they know their marketplace, they are tapped into the right audience, they know how to negotiate, and they know how to get those properties sold for the best prices. It isn't easy to sell in the higher-priced areas. There are fewer available buyers as the price tag goes up and, as that happens, the chance of not selling goes up as well. In addition, there are more expenses involved. The financing tends to be tricky, and often the clients involved are more sophisticated and demanding.

In my area, the majority of expired and cancelled listings in the top quartile in price are not listed by experienced, top agents. These homes don't sell because average agents tend to fumble the higher-end marketplace. These agents also tend to discount their commissions, which can be seen in the MLS. Selling a home at a higher price point is just harder. It shouldn't be left to an agent without experience.

An experienced agent will negotiate a better selling price, or simply walk away from a listing if the seller's expectations are too high. A great agent will use everything they've got and then some to make the sale happen. In the higher-priced market, hiring the right agent is much more important.

Somewhat surprisingly, many sellers don't ask about commissions at all. But many agents feel like it's going to be an issue, so they quickly drop their rate. They just offer a discount. Some agents drop their fee when asked something as simple as "What's your commission?" You might want to consider not hiring an agent who folds that easily. They might blow your sale too.

Some time ago, I interviewed to sell a $2 million home in San Marino, California, one of the most exclusive neighborhoods in Southern California. Nothing had sold in this neighborhood for under $1 million in the past ten years. I was the third agent interviewed. The seller, let's call him Wayne, was a real estate litigator, and during the interview Wayne told me that he sues agents for a living. I think he actually snickered when he said that. As you might guess, that was intimidating. During our conversation, Wayne and his wife asked what commission I charged.

I replied with my standard commission rate and told them that I split this commission with the buyer's agent, so that the agent is incentivized before looking at the listings with discounted commission offerings. I said I always negotiate my commission the way I negotiate a home sale. What they said next was interesting.

Wayne and his wife told me that an hour before I arrived, they had interviewed two top agents. They were a two-person team from a competing brokerage. These two agents outsell almost everyone in town. They told Wayne they'd agree to a commission rate one percentage point lower than what I was charging. I congratulated the sellers and asked them how they were able to negotiate two top agents down on their commission. Wayne said that the agents simply offered them the discount. *There was no negotiation.* Wayne and his wife had merely asked what commission percentage they would charge, and the duo offered a discount right out of the gate. I couldn't help but say, "Ouch."

At that moment, Wayne realized what had happened, and his eyes went wide. He told me he didn't like how the agent folded so quickly, and now that he thought about it, he was concerned that this duo would negotiate the sale of the house the same way.

Wayne was probably right. Maybe the agent duo assumed they would have to discount the commission because Wayne was an intimidating attorney. The duo knew they would have to compete with the multiple agents that Wayne and his wife were interviewing.

In defense of my commission rate, I also explained that a slightly higher buyer's agent commission will entice more agents to show their house. It can provide a stronger escrow, since the agent wouldn't be enticed to show their clients another home (so the agent can make more commission dollars). Wayne and his wife agreed and were happy to sign with me.

I wound up getting three offers on their home. We actually sold the home over the asking price, which no other top agents believed we could achieve. The home was also what we call a tough house to sell. It was a two-story, 2,500-square-foot house that had only one bathroom downstairs. It was a half-bath that was only accessible through the laundry room and a bedroom. Still, the good commission made it so much easier. I remember, as I was touring the backyard with the buyer's agent who won the contract, she told me she "loved the commission."

The clients trusted common sense, and everyone was happy with the result. Wayne and I became friends, and we've seen several baseball games together from his seats at Dodger Stadium. He always buys the Dodger dogs because, as he says, I made him a lot of money.

COMMISSION BREATH

Here is something to be aware of, and it's not necessarily bad breath—though it's almost as bad. In the industry, we call it "commission breath." You might "smell" it when you meet a pushy agent. It's because they want that commission so badly that they're drooling with sales pitches.

Don't mistake pushiness with success. The stereotypical agent will be pushy, and a good agent will try to "close" you. After all, the most successful agents know how to close transactions. Keep in mind, there are limits to pushiness, and there should be a good balance. Don't be offended if an agent even subtly tries to "close" you. After all, you might want to hire an agent who knows how to close a deal!

As new agents we are often reminded that our jobs are as simple as ABC (Always Be Closing). Young or inexperienced agents will try to "close" sellers by encouraging them to sign a listing as quickly as possible. However, a better agent will let a seller review all the paperwork before signing, ask a lot of questions, and offer a common-sense plan of action. The process should be collaborative and designed to get you to your goal. And it should never be under pressure.

"Always Be Closing" was immortalized in the movie *Glengarry Glen Ross*. Do you remember the scene with actor Alec Baldwin playing Blake, the heavy-handed new sales manager, who comes into a real estate sales office meeting to tell the salesmen what their jobs are? He tells them that if they don't sell more, they'll be fired. During that scene, Jack Lemmon's character pours himself a cup of coffee at the back of the office and gets yelled at.

"Put that coffee down! Coffee is for closers only!"

It's the best real estate movie quote ever. It's ruthless. At the beginning of the meeting, Baldwin's character flips the chalkboard around to reveal in big letters "A, B, C." Baldwin then says it three times: "Always. Be. Closing."

As entertaining and stereotypical as that scene is, it isn't the reality of sales meetings today, at least not at the hundreds I've been to. Sometimes, I wish the Alec Baldwin character was my sales manager; it would scare half of the agents out of the business! Today's sales managers are not so rough. Yes, the agent needs to close. That's why we are called salespeople. No, the process doesn't need to be a high-pressure, commission-breath fiasco. Sellers should set the pace.

BREATHING ROOM

> **SELLER MISTAKE**
> Allowing yourself to be pushed into signing a contract with an agent.

Most agents bring paperwork to the first appointment and try and get you to sign on right away. If you are uncomfortable signing, they will encourage you to sign anyway. They will tell you to keep the paperwork at your house overnight and they'll come by the next day to pick it up. Alternatively, the agent will encourage you to sign it, and tell you they will tear it up the next day if you change your mind. These tactics play to the fact that most people don't want to go that far down the track only to stop the train. The agent knows this. These are standard sales tactics that we've been trained in.

Unless you are truly desperate (and no one should be when selling a house), you shouldn't sign anything until you're fully informed, totally convinced, and have interviewed at least three agents. A good agent will provide you with their listing paperwork prior to the appointment, or at least leave it for you to review on your own. They won't be pushy. They'll give you room to breathe.

When I arrive for an appointment, I tell the owners that I'm there to make sure we are a good fit. I give them as much information as possible so they can make the best possible decision. I tell them I didn't bring the listing contract paperwork so that they can breathe easy. If they really want to sign with me, they can. We can take care of it on my laptop with digital signatures, or I can email it to them to review.

My colleagues think I'm nuts, and they tell me I'm losing out on potential contract signings by being so nice. I don't believe that. I don't think I've ever lost out by not bringing the paperwork, and I've never had a homeowner tell me I wasn't a good salesperson because I didn't bring the listing contract. I only bring my paperwork in the rare instance that someone specifically tells me they want it so they can get the process started as soon as possible. Those are usually my repeat clients, or strong referrals.

HOW LONG IS YOUR LISTING CONTRACT?

Along with negotiating commissions and price, a very important item that many sellers fail to negotiate is the *length* of the contract. Most sellers believe that agents want long-term listing contracts, and that's correct. Sellers also often believe that no agent will take short-term listings. That's incorrect.

> **SELLER MISTAKE**
>
> Thinking you must be locked into a long-term contract with your agent.

A typical agent will tell you that their broker requires a six-month or even a one-year listing. Over the last twenty plus years, I've worked at three of the largest brokerages in the U.S., and they've all advised agents to ask the seller to sign for as long a term as possible, while also letting them know that we will accept short listings. I've taken ten-day listings. I've taken two-month listings. I've also taken much longer listings. When you deal with professionals, they will get the job done. The length of the contract is *always* negotiable and should be reasonable to both parties. Never let an agent tell you otherwise.

Most top agents will work short-term. Real professionals will understand (and explain to you) that if they do everything they've promised, they can always extend the listing contract.

Most people don't like to negotiate. That's why they hire someone to do it for them. They don't like how it feels, especially when they're negotiating with the person who is going to negotiate for their home in the future. Some sellers think it will come back to bite them later—it's quite the contrary. I love it when a seller negotiates with me. I respect it. It will almost always uncover the type of sale you'll have.

Always ask. Always negotiate.

8

A BEAUTY CONTEST AND A PRICE WAR

The five main reasons a house doesn't sell are as follows.

1. The price

2. The agent hired

3. The marketing

4. The condition of the home

5. The location

These reasons are also in the order of things that the sellers can control. The seller can always control the asking price and can never control the location. It turns out that it is a beauty contest and a price war when it comes to selling a house.

Most agents will approach a home listing by looking at "comps" (comparable sale listings) to determine the price. They'll get decent photos, write a good description, and roll out the standard marketing (MLS, digital ads, email blasts, etc.). Some will even plant a St. Joseph statue and say a prayer (it works)! However, even if sellers have done all the right things, found a top agent, and crunched the numbers, there's no guarantee their asking price will get them the SOLD sign.

When agents take a listing, they know they're about to enter that home into a beauty contest. Most of those passing judgment will see pictures of that home online. The more drawbacks that are visible in the photos, fewer buyers will show up. Buyers will quickly determine whether your home is worth the price, whether it has what they are seeking, and whether it is appealing enough to take the next step—an appointment for a showing. That's the contest and, unfortunately, many agents (and sellers) don't know how to win it. Most homes do not sell quickly. In normal markets, most never see an offer over the asking price.

How do I know? Here's some eye-opening data: According to the 2020 NAR Generational Trends Report, 55% of homes do not sell at their asking price, and 40% of all homeowners reduce their price at least once. Here in California, just under 50% of all homes sold over the last decade received more than one offer. According to CAR, during that same time period, only one in five homes sold above their final asking price. Our last sobering statistic is from NAR's 2020 Home Buyers and Sellers Generational Trends Report which states that "*40% of all listings take 5 weeks or longer to sell, and most only had one bidder.*" No amount of marketing will sell an overpriced property. When everything else is done correctly, and you're not making big mistakes, it is usually the asking price that stops you from getting sold. Like I said, in addition to being a beauty contest, it's also a price war.

SELLER MISTAKE

Not having an honest discussion with your agent about pricing at the very beginning.

How do you avoid these kinds of problems? Well, an honest pricing conversation should occur when you sign the listing contract with your agent. This might be followed by an uncomfortable discussion to explain what happens if the market doesn't react the way everyone hopes. What if you can't sell by the time you have to move out? What if no offers are forthcoming? Agents are likely to avoid answering these questions during the selling period, so, you, the seller, should bring them up during the interview. Start by being objective.

"TOP FIVE" LISTS

When I see a home for the first time, I try to ascertain the *top five selling points*, as well as the *top five challenges* that might dissuade buyers. Actually, as a home seller, it's helpful to perform this assessment yourself before you even start to interview agents. Top agents will have sharp eyes and will figure the top fives out quickly. The selling points your agent highlights should be the pillars of the marketing strategy, so listen for them carefully.

Know Your Home's Selling Points

Homes that are in the best condition, new or newer homes, homes with great character, homes with great layouts, those that have the best location, that have the best amenities, flow, light, and room to expand, are typically the homes that will sell for the most amount of money in the shortest amount of time. Remember, it's a beauty contest. If you don't have at least five strong selling points from the list below, your home will take more time to sell. And probably need a lower asking price. Here is a list of selling points.

- Location
- Recent upgrades
- Quality of construction
- Square footage
- Enough beds/baths
- Architectural significance
- Quality of the school district
- Layout and flow
- Outdoor space
- Natural light
- Garage
- Storage space
- Room to expand/Size of lot

Know Your Home's Challenges

Every home has challenges, too, and it's important to hear how your agent will sell "around them." If the home needs improvements, then sellers need to know the easiest ways to maximize value. Perhaps they need to make repairs, update the paint palette, or add new appliances, countertops, window coverings, or flooring. If the home has a challenging floor plan, then the agent should help buyers visualize how removing a few walls could greatly enhance the flow. Experienced agents should be able to prioritize the top five concerns and give cost estimates for modifications without having to drag contractors in to give bids.

SELLER MISTAKE
Not being objective about your home's challenges.

Sometimes homeowners are not aware of how serious their home's flaws might appear to buyers. Agents need to be tactful yet honest when explaining such flaws, particularly for those that cannot be easily modified. Perhaps the home has only one bathroom, and additional bathrooms would be difficult to add. Maybe desirable architectural features have been stripped. It could be that the garage is too small, or maybe the kitchen has no pantry.

Other challenges include proximity to power lines, zoning issues, foundation concerns, or an outdated style. One way that agents handle these challenges is to point out that many of the homes nearby have the same issues. Such observations make buyers more comfortable with these concerns.

In some areas of California, bad *feng shui* (how the energy forces harmonize individuals with their surrounding environment) can also be a significant deterrent for a buyer.

And then there's location. Location, location, location. It's a mantra for a reason. The perception of a home's status and value can be strongly affected by the neighborhood and community features around it. You can change just about everything about a house, except its location. Top agents will assure sellers that when they are talking to buyers, they have ways to couch the location challenge within the entire list of pros and cons about a home. These agents can learn some of the history and culture of a neighborhood, so they are prepared for difficult location questions. They can find information about neighborhood improvements and what's in store for the community's future. Whatever the challenges, the skills and expertise of a good agent are indispensable for a seller.

Keep in mind, even if you are winning the beauty contest, there is still the price war.

PRICE IT RIGHT

While you really don't have control over the market price, you do have control over your asking price. However, many sellers and agents bungle the asking price, and it winds up being a big, expensive mistake. After all, 55% of all listings do not sell at their asking price, and that figure doesn't include the homes that didn't sell at all. Having a price that a buyer trusts as reasonable is half the battle.

As I mentioned earlier in this chapter, most agents like to "run comps." They do that to provide a comparative market analysis (CMA) and show you how your home compares with other properties, as well as how quickly a home goes into contract (days on market, or DOM). However, comps don't tell the whole story of the market. An *absorption rate analysis* is a tool that most agents have access to but do not provide for their clients. This analysis is usually in graph form and shows how many and how quickly like-kind properties have been on the market, in contract, and closed

SELLER MISTAKE
Pricing your home too high.

on a month-to-month basis. This analysis shows how quickly properties are going on the market, going into escrow, and getting sold. It shows what the historical seasons have looked like, and where the market has leaned toward—a buyer's market or a seller's market. It also shows what percentage of homes are selling over their asking prices, and how many months of inventory for your type of property is out there. If you know where the market is going, it can be much easier to determine the right price.

I tell my clients to price their home like it's a good deal, but not a steal. Selling a home is about motivation and engagement, and price is a powerful instrument to inspire both, as long as the agent is doing everything else correctly. Nevertheless, the asking price needs to be close to market price, based on comparables, absorption rates, and where the market is going. After all, no one knows the marketplace better than a motivated buyer.

Must I Sell if Someone Offers Me My Asking Price?

This is a question a lot of my clients have. Generally, the answer is no. However, it does depend on what your listing contract says. Most, if not all, listing contracts created by your state Association of Realtors® will stipulate that if you receive a full-price offer, you will act in good faith to respond to it. Keep in mind, responding doesn't mean you have to accept it. The typical listing contract isn't an agreement to sell. It is an agreement to have a certain agent and their brokerage to market and negotiate a sale, and to pay them a commission once the sale is completed.

If you get your asking price immediately, maybe you've done well. But there's still a chance that you've left money on the table. Can you get more if you wait a few days? Most home buyers will wait a few days. What about the other sales comparables? Are they selling immediately? Are you priced too low or just right? This is another instance where a local, experienced agent can provide answers.

High-end sales can be tricky, even for the pros. It isn't uncommon for agents to ask their colleagues (yes, their competitors) for price feedback on a home that's about to go on the market. Be open to having your agent bring other agents through to see your home before going on the MLS. Getting feedback can be a powerful tool for the seller and can create some market buzz. It isn't a sign of weakness. It's smart.

SELLER MISTAKE

Not listening to the market about the price of your home.

Let the Market Speak!

When a home goes on the open market, industry veterans like to say, "The market will speak." What does that mean? If you don't receive any offers on your home, then the market has spoken, and it's usually telling you that your home is overpriced.

The best and the highest number of buyers will see your home within the first few days and weeks of going on the market.

Statistics prove that the faster a home sells, the higher the price it will sell for. The opposite is also true. The longer a home takes to sell, it generally means that its sales price goes down because there are fewer buyers and less leverage to get the best price. The entire marketplace is engaged at the beginning of a listing. As time goes on, it is hard to get attention, and when buyers see that your home hasn't sold, they tend to think that the home clearly isn't worth its asking price. You might be saying to yourself that you have lots of time, that you aren't in a hurry, and that you can wait. Unfortunately, there isn't much data to support that strategy if you want the highest price. The fact is, staying on the market longer seldom gets you more money. It just doesn't work that way. Unless the market is going up, and you have the time and a high tolerance for risk, you are almost always better off selling sooner rather than later. Time works against you.

Multiple Offers and Bidding Wars

Some sellers' agents sometimes suggest a very low asking price to entice buyers. However, sellers need to be careful not to sell too quickly in this scenario. The market will always dictate the price as the offers come in, especially if the sales process is handled correctly. If you get offers within the first hours or days, then you will probably get more offers if you wait a little longer before responding to anyone. Also, be careful with your expectations about multiple offers, bidding wars, and selling over asking price, even in a hot market. That dreamy scenario we often see on HGTV isn't automatic.

Having twenty, thirty, or even forty offers on a home is something that many agents wear like a badge of honor. All this means is that they priced the home way too low—which can be risky and expensive for sellers. Fielding offers isn't easy, given the amount of paperwork involved. Most offers are fifteen to twenty pages long, and with the barrage of emails and incoming calls, agents can become overwhelmed. Each offer can take twenty to forty minutes to present to a seller. It isn't easy to get organized, negotiate effectively, and communicate under these circumstances. Even with ten offers on a home, my phone is constantly ringing, and I'm fielding at least a hundred emails a day. Pricing a home correctly and not having to handle a huge number of offers makes the selling process much more likely to run smoothly and successfully. When there are a lot of offers, it's tough to communicate to the buyers' agents, and for them, no news is bad news. It's just too easy for a buyer to get less enthusiastic unless they think they have a real shot.

Getting a lot of offers doesn't necessarily mean market price was hit. Hitting the market price with a lot of offers can be tough for a number of reasons. With so many offers because of a too low asking price, it can make it difficult to get the best buyers to stretch higher to reach the actual market price. In situations like this, it's common to have buyers bow out during the process, especially in a bidding war. Some serious buyers don't want to be a part of a feeding frenzy. They get scared away. Even if a property is priced artificially low, buyers tend to decide before bidding what their price limit is. Therefore, many of those low offers are a waste of time for everyone. Buyers and their agents want communication and feedback to stay engaged. If the listing agent is overwhelmed with superfluous buyers, there is less attention given to the better buyers who will go higher.

SELLER MISTAKE
Pricing your home too low.

The right balance of offers depends on the marketplace. A great goal for a typical home is to receive about five offers within around two weeks to two months. Higher-end or specialty homes usually take longer to sell because the pool of buyers is limited.

Aside from getting to market price, getting multiple offers allows leverage for the seller to negotiate better terms, such as the close of escrow and shorter buyer contingencies. Keep in mind that after buyers have done their inspections, they normally will ask for some sort of concession (repair, credit, or price reduction). It's easier to say no to that when the buyer knows you have a backup buyer. It also depends on how strong a negotiator your agent is (you read Chapter 7, didn't you?).

If the asking price happens to be the price where offers come in, and if you are satisfied that you haven't sold too quickly and have marketed it the way I've described in this book, then go ahead and sign on the dotted line. Congratulations. You and your agent have done well!

Pocket Price vs. Market Price

Too often, when sellers' agents are allowed to represent buyers, or to pre-market the home, they don't post the listing on the MLS. Instead, they go to their own buyers, or to small portals, perhaps a newspaper ad, their own website, or they rely on a For Sale sign. By putting the listing in their "pocket" they're disregarding the largest audience, the MLS, and they're not cooperating with other agents.

> ## SELLER MISTAKE
> Thinking that a "Pocket Listing" is good for you, the seller.

The phrase "pocket listing" traces back to the very beginning of the real estate brokerage business. When agents had a signed listing, they wouldn't market it; they would put that paperwork in their pockets and call their own clients, never exposing the listing to the entire marketplace. Pocket listings almost always benefit the buyer and the dual agent. It's obvious that the pocket price is almost always lower than market price. It goes against common sense to think otherwise.

"BUYING A LISTING" (IT'S NOT WHAT YOU THINK)

Agents "buy a listing" when they tell the seller they can get an inflated price. In this business, you can always find someone who will tell you what you want to hear. In this case, I'm referring to a higher price for your home. Too often, a seller will interview several agents and settle on the agent who comes up with the highest selling price. The seller thinks, "Wow, this agent is so optimistic and convincing, they must know what they're talking about."

The agent hasn't bought your house, but the agent has *bought* you with an unrealistically high price expectation.

You see, buying a listing is not risky for an agent. Agents know that if the home doesn't sell, they will just ask the seller for a price reduction. They may try to do as many open houses as possible while they're at it, and why not? The agent knows that they priced the home too high, so they might as well make the best of a difficult situation. Again, NAR *says* agents should use listings to get more leads, so why not take an overpriced listing? No agent wants to be the one who disappoints sellers with an honest price estimate that happens to be the lowest. And suppose another agent can reasonably justify a high price with hard numbers and can explain the pricing strategy with common sense. In that case, perhaps, the agent recommending the highest price is the one to go with. Perhaps. But far too often, agents are hungry for listings, so they give inflated prices just to get the client on board. Honest agents consider this a dirty trick that they know rarely pays off for a seller. While it's impossible to know how many listings are "bought" by an agent, a good portion of those never sell. The listing expires, or it gets cancelled. The fact that almost half of all homes need a price reduction to sell says a lot about overly hungry agents (and sellers).

Buying a listing is a constant source of annoyance to good agents, and it isn't fair to home sellers. In fact, it can be punitive, and the practice is borderline illegal, but in this selling game it is very often too difficult to prove malicious intent.

Sometimes a seller wants or needs a certain price, or perhaps believes that a high asking price makes the home appear to be worth more. Perhaps buyers will agree. That is a rare outcome. This is sort of like overpricing a diamond, or a car. There is certainly some logic to that. But it's risky, you must admit. This is called "trying to set the market," and when a seller engages in this, the effect is usually short-lived. Most sellers, whose home listings either expired or were cancelled, will tell you that their asking price was too high, and they didn't know that until it was too late. When the listing goes back on the market with a new price, this sends the message to the market that the home was probably overpriced the first time around.

> ## SELLER MISTAKE
>
> Thinking that overpricing your home will have the best results for you.

"But," asks a seller, "wouldn't buyers give offers on overpriced homes—offers for what they think they're worth? Heck, if they really like a house, shouldn't they bid for it?" Isn't that a logical strategy and a good reason to start with a high price?

You are not going to like the answer. It just doesn't work like that in residential real estate. Buyers will *rarely* write a low offer on what they or their agents perceive as an overpriced home. They think it's a waste of time, they don't want to insult the seller, and they think their offer will go nowhere. They tend to assume the seller is asking too much and that those sellers are clueless about the reality of the market. If this strategy worked, it would be commonplace.

CHASING THE MARKET DOWN

In other cases, agents don't even *know* they've made the mistake of pricing a home too high. Maybe the seller insisted on starting high. Maybe the agent wasn't aware of the comps. Eventually, however, everyone will realize the mistake. There might be fewer showings than normal or none at all. There might be low offers, or none at all. If other agents tell your listing agent that the home seems overpriced, your agent needs to listen, and you do too. Is your agent giving you feedback from buyers and other agents? You should be hearing it every time the home is shown. Buyer's agents usually love to give feedback. If your agent complains that she isn't getting feedback about a home, then tell her to call everyone who showed the house and ask for it, and also have her line up a handful of successful agents from her office to offer feedback as well.

Depending on your marketplace, if you're not getting showings or decent offers in the first few weeks (or perhaps months), then often the next step is to ask for more marketing and to correct the asking price. Assuming you've done everything suggested in this book, then it's usually a matter of time versus money. Can you stay on the market longer or must you adjust the price, effectively chasing the market down?

Agents know that even if a home doesn't sell within the first month, they'll still have the listing, and all they'll need to do is get the seller to reduce the price. They keep reducing the price until they get action. At that point you are chasing after fewer and fewer buyers, and buyers will sense that there's blood in the water, which will hopefully force a sale.

There's a problem with this kind of strategy. When you reduce the price of a home, it causes the seller to miss the best buyers, and it's more likely that the home will sell under market value. If you were a buyer and saw the price dropping, wouldn't you think that there's an opportunity for you to buy the home at a better (lower) price since there are fewer buyers?

Homes that have been on the market for two to three times the average selling time usually have at least one price reduction before they sell, and they usually don't sell at the asking price.

Another problem with chasing the market is that an overpriced home typically results in the seller working with only one buyer. That means no bidding war or backup offers, and little leverage for the home seller. It gets worse. The buyer usually knows there are no backup offers and tends to grind down the price during the sales process. It also becomes more and more difficult to negotiate favorable terms such as shorter buyer contingency timeframes and concessions. The three big buyer contingencies are inspection of the property and its disclosure paperwork, loan qualification, and bank appraisal. Using these contingencies, buyers can and will try to negotiate a reduction in price, a credit, and even repairs. The shorter these contingencies are, the better it is for the seller. Otherwise, it can be a horrible situation for a seller.

WHY TELL THE SELLER?

While some agents will walk away from an overpriced home listing, many will not. Why should they? They'll be able to promote themselves and maybe they'll be able to meet other potential sellers and buyers to further their business. Maybe everyone will get lucky. When there aren't any showings or offers, the agent can always tell the seller that the marketplace suddenly got a little wonky. For the typical agent, there are a lot of potential benefits, even if the home doesn't get an offer. So, why tell the seller?

If you're an agent reading this book, please remember that it is okay to say no. When you buy a listing, you are putting an innocent homeowner's equity at risk, and it will be a waste of time for everyone (unless you just hammer them for price drops and use their home to selfishly market yourself). If sellers won't take your advice, then tell them you aren't the right agent for them. They can decide to list with somebody else. Say, "Call me if it doesn't work out."

As a seller, how do you prevent an agent from buying your listing? Quite simply, study the market and ask a lot of questions. Again, your agent should be able to explain a pricing strategy that you fully understand. Don't let him try to sway you with jargon. Look at comparables and ask for a market absorption analysis. This way you can get a good estimate of how long your home will take to sell based on the sale of other homes. Better yet, ask the agent, "Are you trying to buy my listing?" This is a shock of a question for any agent. An ethical and experienced local agent will always be able to answer with multiple reasons and strategies behind their recommended asking price.

For high-end listings there can be a big incentive for an agent to buy a listing. Depending on the marketplace, location of the property, or its provenance, a very high listing price can garner the agent more publicity and exposure than they could ever pay for. Imagine having a listing that is worth $10 million, but the listing price is $20 million. For a few thousand dollars in marketing and strategic PR placements, the agent can get exposure for themselves that would normally cost tens of thousands of dollars. Imagine, the agent gets their name in *The Wall Street Journal*, *The New York Times*, or the *Los Angeles Times*, or all three. Like I mentioned earlier, it would be foolish for an agent to not use their listing to get other leads. You should be asking, is this good for the seller?

SELLER MISTAKE
Letting the agent use your listing to advance their best interests, not yours.

Usually not, as we've all read the stories of how long these types of properties take to sell, and they almost always sell for below their asking prices. I just think the seller needs to be fully aware of the situation.

USING YOUR HOME TO SELL OTHER PEOPLE'S HOMES

Just because you put your house on the market at a high price and have buyers coming to view it, that doesn't always mean you have truly interested buyers. One of the oldest tricks in the real estate book is something that really upsets sellers: agents using your home to sell other people's homes. Yes, they really do this. I'm sure your agent never told you this one.

It goes like this. An agent brings a buyer to your house and says to their buyer, "Look at this price. I know you aren't interested in this house. Let's just look at it to compare." Or they tell them, "Look at this house. They are asking $700,000 and the one down the street is very similar. They're only asking $650,000. Let's look at both, but the $650,000 house looks like the better deal." This probably *sounds* unethical. But it's done all the time. It's called comparison shopping.

My family and I love to vacation in the Lake Arrowhead area, a beautiful countryside destination only an hour and a half's drive from Los Angeles. Lake Arrowhead's lakefront properties with docks usually sell for at least $2 million. A few have sold for close to $6 million. However, for the past several years, I've noticed five to ten homes on the market priced at $10 million or more. They almost never sell and have been on the market for three to over five years. They seem to defy reality.

A neighborhood is only a $10 million neighborhood if homes are actually *selling* for $10 million. Agents use those expensive, overpriced homes to sell other homes in those neighborhoods that are priced better. Buyers believe they're getting a great deal when they buy at $6 million while the house next door is priced at $10 million.

Remember: sellers don't set the market. Buyers do. The overpriced listings certainly get a lot of publicity and buyer showings, but they rarely ever sell anywhere close to their lofty asking prices. The greatest number of buyers looking at your home are there in the first days and weeks. If your home is overpriced, almost all will look elsewhere.

On the other hand, if a seller's agent is handling the contest well and the property is priced correctly, a home will sell for market price or even above asking price or appraised price with the best terms. It's all about the price. Period. While a top agent will tell you they've done everything else right, if the asking price was too high, and if you haven't made any other mistakes, then your agent is probably right.

9

THE OPEN HOUSE

An open house is just that. Open. Open to anyone who wants to come. Anyone from a criminal on the street to your ex-wife's snoopy boyfriend. Are you comfortable with that?

When people think of selling real estate, they assume it requires a lot of open houses. Agents want you to believe that they are crucial to a sale. But they are not. While open houses are one of real estate's most traditional customs, they are not that important to actually selling a home. Many agents will defend it to their death, however.

The best source of open house data is from NAR. They tell us, for example, that 52% of all sellers said their agent used open houses to market their home. However, their data is perplexing because it doesn't provide reasons why, or even if, open houses are a key to a sale. It's almost as if NAR purposely does not want anyone to know the truth about open houses. More on this later...

Open houses were once a primary tool for real estate agents selling a home. It was the "big reveal"—the first showing for potential buyers. These days, however, buyers overwhelmingly say open houses are *not* their primary way of finding their dream home—not even close. As a matter of fact, buyers tell us that their first viewing isn't at an open house, nor is it when they walk in the front door for the first time with their agent.

Today's first showing of a home for sale is online, and it's actually been this way for a few decades. Don't let anyone tell you anything different.

I won't tell you just yet that open houses are a waste of time—or potentially worse. For now, I'll let you know what tens of thousands of homebuyers across the nation have been saying for years. You guessed it: *open houses don't sell houses.*

I wish I could tell you the evidence about the effectiveness of open houses for typical home sellers. The problem is that no one has this data because the national and state associations of Realtors® don't ask consumers. We have to make assumptions with purposely limited data.

What do the statistics tell us? NAR said that in 2020, 6% of all buyers found the home they purchased through a sign or an open house sign. Wow. That's 94% unhelpful. What do the statistics tell us about an ordinary open house event? Nothing, because this question isn't asked! Here's another nugget of information from NAR: only 3% of buyers visit an open house. Hmmm.

Let's dig into more stats.

1. NAR's stats include all signs and open houses on existing, *and* newly constructed, *and* FSBO (for sale by owner) homes. (Chapter 6 is all about FSBO-ing.) Yes, all these types of sellers are put into one single statistic. Maybe you don't think this is a big deal. Read on.

2. Every single day is basically an open house at a new development. In 2020 the percentage of new home sales in the United States was 13%. According to the State of Home Builder Marketing Report 2020, 69% of American developers rely on signage and billboards to literally drive traffic to their home sites—where they have sales staff ready to give model home tours every day. However, we don't know the effectiveness of open houses just for new homes because NAR doesn't provide this data. Wouldn't it be useful to know the answer to this?

3. The FSBO sellers were grouped into the open house statistic as well. According to NAR, FSBO sellers' number two marketing tool is hosting an open house (number one is signage).

NAR or CAR doesn't even provide the stats as to whether open houses generate more sales or increase the sales price. Is that intentional? Wouldn't everyone love to know whether open houses generate more offers and/or help drive up the price? Sometimes the absence of something is just as significant as its presence. Not providing these statistics is telling.

NAR does provide some news regarding the success of open houses. For the largest demographic of buyers, 7% found their agents through an open house visit, while 3% of sellers found their agents this way. *That's how agents get 10% of their business!* Did you know that's ten times better than print ads, and more than a hundred times better than emails?

Many Realtors® feel that the data from our trade group is purposely incomplete to benefit our own members. After all, it clearly benefits agents to tell their sellers that open houses are effective. Again, FSBOs account for only about 6% of all sales.

So, to summarize, when you remove the new homes and FSBOs, the number of sales that happen from open houses is, at best, minuscule.

IF OPEN HOUSES DON'T BENEFIT THE SELLER, THEN WHY HAVE ONE?

Have you ever really thought about the ways agents get their business? Good looks, signs, ads, and emails don't cut it. Face time is the answer. Face time that often comes by way of your open house. That's how many agents *build their* businesses. It's not how your house gets sold.

What about a virtual open house? I'm not a fan. It's a live stream of an agent walking through a house with others on the video call, but the buyer cannot control or record it. What's better are pre-recorded video or a 360 degree 3D virtual tour (Matterport is the market leader) since both can be viewed any time. Video is like photography; you can show only what you want to show. But 3D virtual tours show the good and the bad, and consumers spend a lot of time viewing these tours and for good reason. More on this in Chapter 10.

On NAR's website, there is a page titled "Media Hooks for Realtor® Open Houses." It's meant "to help you pitch" open houses to the media. In the past, NAR promoted a "Realtor® Nationwide Open House Weekend." But as inventory went down over the years, and because of the ineffectiveness of open houses, they dropped the event. Different states and regions still held their own "Open House Weekends," where agents are encouraged to open their inventory to the public. But why?

Most Realtors® are recognizing that the traditional open house will continue to sharply decline in effectiveness and use because of the 2020 pandemic. Again, with the pandemic, open houses went virtual since in-person events were discouraged by local health departments and consumers.

Virtual showings and digital marketing increased tremendously as random in-person visits were banned by health officials. After reading through this chapter, you might agree that open houses will likely be used less over time. Still, the pandemic didn't put an end to open houses for good, and you'll soon see why.

THE BENEFITS OF OPEN HOUSES

If open houses are so ineffective at selling homes, why have one? That's because agents profit from them. They are fantastic platforms to display agents' talents and their brokerage's brand. In an open house, your home becomes what we in the business call a "lead-generation tool." They get to use your front room to market themselves, live and in person! Sure, while they say they are marketing the house, agents know better. This business is all about getting leads: buyer leads, seller leads, and referral leads. These leads help the agent and rarely bring offers to the homeowner. Even Realtor.com says, "Your house is the agent's best free marketing platform around." Google it.

> ## SELLER MISTAKE
> Thinking that you are the one who benefits from an open house, not your agent.

I have heard many agents say that a crowd at an open house creates a sense of urgency and of competition. That's a very valid point. But, do buyers really need to see other people to get a sense of urgency?

I don't do open houses, and I can easily create a sense of urgency in an honest phone conversation with agents. If buyers are interested in a house, they almost always have their agent call the listing agent.

Before the pandemic, one of my competitors in Pasadena held open houses every single weekend. If you met this agent at one of his listings, you'd notice his big notebook of flyers for properties he has sold over the years. Of course, he hands out flyers at every open house. It's "all about him"—not about the home. He sells a lot of real estate by using open houses as his primary lead-generation tool. Some call him "Mr. Open House." He will tell you that open houses work.

Few agents will admit to the fact that open houses are ineffective for sellers. Most will still tell you how important it is to have one. We know that buyers like to go to open houses to get a feel for the area, to get a sense of the market, and to see what styles they like or dislike. Doesn't everyone love looking at decorating and design ideas? A house that's open to everyone is perfect for that. However, when buyers get serious, they overwhelmingly say they use the internet and their agent to select a home.

Brokerage managers routinely tell their agents that every listing should generate two qualified buyer or seller leads. What do you think is the best way to get face-to-face with those leads? It's a well-known industry fact that prospective sellers go to open houses so they can get an idea of the marketplace and to meet agents. Ask any experienced agent: weekends are for leads!

Most agents still rely on open houses, which is a testament to the fact that agents are mostly focused on their own lead generation. The Real Estate Marketing Analysis Survey by REAL Trends, a real estate consulting and research firm, asked agents what they invested in to promote their brand. Seventy-one percent of agents responded with "open houses." Old habits die hard, which is why we heard a lot about virtual open houses during the pandemic. As the world opened up, the industry pushed to get open houses going again.

MOTIVATED BUYERS DON'T NEED OPEN HOUSES

Because most buyers find their homes on the internet, most first showings happen online. The second showing is when the buyer steps into your home. If the house's online presence is done well, a buyer will want to see the home in person. While there are tons of looky-loos, a real buyer is motivated. They'll call their agent and make an appointment. Not having an open house won't stop a motivated buyer. No buyer has ever said, "I didn't buy that home because they didn't have an open house."

You don't need an open house to find buyers for your home because most of the people who come to an open house aren't motivated. Targeting unmotivated buyers in the hope of motivating them can work, and we've all heard the stories of someone walking into an open house and deciding right there to buy. Frankly, situations like this are rare and probably less than 0.1% of all sales. If your agent is going to focus on that, then they might as well place ads in the newspaper (see Chapter 10).

Ask anyone who has bought a house recently. They will most likely tell you that when they found a home online and liked what they saw, they made an appointment to see the house. If it had an open house, that's nice. Remember, real buyers make appointments. That's how it has worked on all the homes I've sold.

WHO ACTUALLY DOES THE OPEN HOUSE?

Did you know that in many cases the person handling your open house will *not* be the agent you hired? If you hired an experienced agent, you might see rookie colleagues running the open house so they can meet more people. Newer agents need to get leads and they usually start working with buyers before they graduate to representing sellers. While there is no official data on what percentage of agents holding open houses are rookies, I wouldn't be surprised if it was as high as 50%.

THINGS YOU DON'T WANT TO HEAR

If agents have ever told you that they "want to do open houses every weekend until it sells," or "I want to bring buyers to see your home before we go on the market" or "I have buyers lined up," then those may be dual agents who are likely looking out for their wallet and not yours. They might be more motivated to get their buyer off their plate rather than getting the best deal for a seller.

DUAL AGENCY WITH OPEN HOUSES

Over the course of my career, I've had several agents tell me that because I don't do open houses, I am missing out on opportunities to get leads and to double-end the house. They are 100% correct.

It's easy for an open house agent to say "If you want to write an offer, call your agent. If you want to *get* this house, then you should go through me." Unrepresented buyers often attend open houses and they are, of course, potential new clients for the agent hosting the open house. However, buyers could lose their right to be represented by their own agent if they agree to be represented by the seller's agent. Commission disputes can erupt because the listing broker could refuse to split the commission with the buyer's agent. What a mess.

Buyer Beware

When you've attended an open house, have you seen the sign-in request? Did you know that signing in may actually impede your agent's ability to represent you in buying that house—unless you are willing to pay the commission? Sellers traditionally pay the commission, and it's split between the buyer's and the seller's brokerages. The listing agent could refuse to pay your agent, forcing the seller to pay an additional commission. This situation happens often enough that buyers actually need to be counseled before going to open houses.

If you are a buyer and already have a relationship with an agent, when you go to an open house, it's best to let the open house agent know that you are already working with an agent. Let them know that you don't want to sign in. If the agent requires you to sign in, that's fine. Just be sure to write down the name of your agent next to yours—better yet, include their phone number, too.

WHAT REALLY HAPPENS AT AN OPEN HOUSE?

Visitors at open houses aren't screened. Let me ask you this: how exactly is an agent supposed to screen open house visitors? Signing in upon arrival is not screening. An agent is lucky if half the people who sign in even give their real information. It's all a show. Have you ever heard an agent ask someone to leave or prevent someone from entering? It's rare.

What happens when you allow your agent to walk strangers through your home on a Saturday or Sunday afternoon? First, most visitors will be looky-loos who are attracted to your home while driving to lunch or running errands. Almost everyone acts like a real buyer. Neighbors will also stop by because they know you are probably out of the house, and this is their only chance to see how you live!

Open Houses—An Invitation to Steal

When sellers sign a listing contract, they could be signing away more than they are aware of. Consider this from the CAR contract:

"The broker is not responsible for the loss or damage to personal or real property or persons, whether attributable to the showing of a home, lockbox, or even open houses."

California contracts also state that the brokerage doesn't maintain insurance to protect sellers. Other states' contracts are similar. Do sellers realize this? I've sold over 500 homes and have never known a seller who was aware of this clause before I spelled it out for them.

The following is a typical open house scenario that can quickly turn unmanageable. Imagine an ordinary couple walking into an open house where they meet the agent, the only person there. The agent greets them just inside the door and tells them a little about the house. They thank the agent and say that they are just looking. Then, at the invitation of the agent, they start wandering around.

Now, some agents will follow the couple as they walk around the house. But this can seem a bit too imposing since they just want to look and don't seem too interested in engaging. Also, the agent wants to stay close to the front door in case someone else walks in (maybe a live lead!). The agent decides to give the couple some space, and maybe even lets them go upstairs unattended. What could possibly go wrong? Perhaps you're thinking to yourself, "My agent would never let that happen." Sure.

A common question at an open house is, "May I use the bathroom?" However, you're lucky if the person even asks. Many will use it while the agent is distracted. How do you say "no" to someone who wants to quickly use the bathroom? The owner will never know, right? Also, the agent doesn't know if the people could be potential buyers, and who wants to be rude to a potential buyer? These situations happen often enough, but agents rarely mention them to the homeowner. It gets worse.

The number one item stolen from open houses is prescription medication. And where are prescription meds often located in the home? You got it: in the bathroom. I tell my clients that if they really want an open house, they need to hide all their prescriptions. Meds, along with any other small valuables, are best taken completely out of the home. Better yet, put everything valuable in the trunk of your car and drive away.

If you look at police department websites, you'll usually find regular warnings to homeowners and real estate agents about the risks of holding open houses. The agent promises that they will keep a keen eye on what is going on. However, open houses usually mean opening up an uncontrollable situation that the agent cannot effectively monitor.

If you ask your agent about screening the people who come into your home, their response is usually a combination of the following lines:

- *"I've never had a problem."*
- *"I just know if a person coming into your home is up to no good."*
- *"We never have problems like that in this nice of a neighborhood."*
- *"Oh, I'll watch your house, don't you worry."*

It's incredibly difficult to determine the bad apples (or drug users) by their appearance. Visitors have also been known to hide in closets or basements until the open house ends. Once the agent leaves, the thieves can grab what they want and bolt out the back door. There are also stories about people "casing" open houses, so they can come back later to break in. How can an agent possibly determine if a visitor is there to case the house? The sign-in sheet doesn't cut it. Video in the house or a video doorbell doesn't do it either.

It Gets Dangerous

Open houses are, in fact, so unsafe for agents that Realtor® associations constantly offer open house safety seminars and webinars. In the early 2000s, NAR started promoting "Realtor® Safety Week." It has now morphed into "Realtor® Safety Month"—the whole month of September!

Most agents who reported finding themselves in dangerous situations at open houses were women. In 2020, the typical Realtor® was a 55-year-old female. Many agents team up for safety, and many female agents will have their husband or boyfriend with them (often sitting in a back room reading a book, hoping he won't have to play superhero).

At an open house, criminals know that the agent is isolated and in an unfamiliar setting. In most cases, agents don't know where to run or where potential weapons are located in case of an emergency. For many agents, an open house means their safety is in their own hands.

This business can be harrowing. We spend a lot of time alone in the vacant and occupied homes of strangers. NAR's 2020 Member Safety Report showed that 23% of agents experienced something on the job that "made them fear for their safety." Another 4% of agents said they had been victims of a crime while on the job. These days, agents are taking security seriously. NAR reports that 49% of agents are armed, either with pepper spray, a gun, a knife, or a Taser (in that order). Agents are concerned, and as tough as it is for agents to say "no" to an open house, some are doing just that.

> **SELLER MISTAKE**
>
> Not understanding the danger of letting strangers into your home at an open house.

The Agent's Role in an Open House

As I'm sure you've guessed, I regard open houses, and virtual open houses, as the wrong way to sell a house. However, you still might think that an agent who does an open house is a hard-working agent. Let's do the math. It takes about six hours for an agent to execute an effective open house. They need a bunch of flyers, open house signs strategically placed throughout the neighborhood, perhaps a bit of door knocking, and maybe even some print and online ads.

Open houses also rarely end on time. A visitor almost always shows up right around the end, and that person often happens to be someone who loves to talk. Usually "a talker" walks through the house while I am trying to close up and won't stop talking, often after admitting disinterest in buying the home. Open houses are a lot of effort.

WHAT ELSE TO CONSIDER ABOUT OPEN HOUSES

Perhaps what you've read so far hasn't completely convinced you to avoid having open houses.

If you insist on having an open house, have one and one only, and have it on the first weekend your home goes on the market.

The agent's responsibility for that first open house is to attract as many buyers as possible. Additional open houses can make a seller appear desperate. If your home has been on the market for longer than the average time it takes to sell a home, then an open house suggests to buyers that there's little interest in the property and few offers, if any. You are basically announcing to the world that your home probably has no offers, and, for some reason, you can't sell it. As a result, buyers will think there's a higher chance that the seller will accept a lowball offer. Most honest agents will tell you that the more open houses you do, often the more damaging it will be to the ultimate sales price of your house.

SELLER MISTAKE
Thinking that multiple open houses will help sell your house.

Another alternative to a slew of standard open houses is for your agent to host an open house exclusively for other agents, called a *broker's open*, *broker caravan*, or *broker's preview*. An ambitious seller's agent typically recommends it soon after they list the home. It's a great opportunity for these agents to see as much housing inventory as possible without a lockbox or an appointment.

The goal of the broker's open is to get agents into your house, so they'll spread the word to their buyers. Broker's opens are scheduled Monday through Friday, from late morning to just after lunch, a slow time for a real estate agent. Depending on the market, it can often be more effective to hold the broker's open house up to two weeks after a home goes on the market. A week after you list your house, if you're not seeing the buyer activity you and your agent hoped for, then the broker's open can give you a little boost. The broker's open house for my area is on Thursdays from 10 a.m. to 2 p.m.

However, the broker's open also isn't without its problems. Because there will be signs up in the neighborhood for the broker caravan, looky-loos and neighbors tend to stop by. There isn't always a flow of agents coming. I recommend asking your agent how effective a broker's open house is in your area. In northern Los Angeles, for example, the broker caravans aren't always well attended, nor very successful at attracting good brokers. This is because the business has changed; buyers now shop online more and more.

JUST SAY NO

It has become clear that an open house is an ineffective, passive, and even dangerous approach to selling a home. The data supporting this is overwhelming. As an agent, I don't need to incorporate open houses into my business model because I have other ways to generate business. Simply opening doors to random passersby in the hopes that they will buy is a mistake.

10

BAD MARKETING STRATEGIES

HOW EFFECTIVE IS THE FOR SALE SIGN FOR A TYPICAL HOME SELLER?

Well, this is embarrassing. NAR and I can't give you a concise answer to this question. In NAR's 143-page report there is no data specifically given about the effectiveness of a For Sale sign with pre-owned homes that were sold with a real estate agent (which is about 90% of all transactions). The information just isn't there. I know, it's ridiculous. Nevertheless, they did leave us some clues.

As you know, in 2020, NAR said that just 6% of all buyers discovered the home they eventually purchased by seeing a sign:

Signs for an open house,

A For Sale sign on either a new or pre-owned home,

A For Sale sign at a FSBO, and

"Other" signs, like developer billboards.

Yes, they combined every type of sign into one stat. I thought that something was missing. Why would they do that? Why wouldn't they ask a buyer or seller a simple question: Did a For Sale sign by your agent result in the sale or purchase of your home? It seems to be a sensible stat for everyone to know. However, it isn't, and you will soon find out why. Let's dig into the data.

When we look at the largest buyer of real estate's demographic (29–38 years old), the success rate for a For Sale sign number drops to 5% effectiveness. Not surprisingly, buyers under 29 years old came in at only 2%. These percentages (6%, 5%, and 2%) include both new *and* pre-owned homes with either For Sale signs, open house signs, *or* "other" signs like billboards, with and without an agent (FSBOs).

According to CAR's 2020 consumer survey, most buyers found their home online or through their agent. "Word of mouth" registered at a whopping 7% effectiveness. Wait a second. Word of mouth is more effective than all types of signage for all types of properties, with or without an agent? Come on!

Long before the internet, For Sale signs and other gimmicks were crucial to a home seller's success. The agent was the gatekeeper of information. If you wanted to know what was on the market, you had to get a newspaper, go to an agent, look at open houses, or drive neighborhoods looking for signs. You had to call the phone number on the sign, which would lead to more business for the agent. Now, the tables have turned. The agents no longer control the information. We are now service providers. According to NAR, over 90% of buyers are going online for their home search.

For me, signs haven't been very effective. I can count on one hand—well, actually, three fingers—how many buyers found and bought my listing because my For Sale sign was in the yard. So, for me, the For Sale sign is less than 1% effective. No one knows the actual numbers. As I mentioned earlier, it's a simple question for NAR to ask. For an unknown reason (wink, wink), they don't ask. Why?

Because signage is so important *to the agent and to the brokerage.* It's free advertising. Agents want leads! Why on Earth would NAR and agents want sellers to know that the sign is almost totally ineffective, or worse?

I mentioned earlier that NAR is a trade group, and the primary purpose of a trade group is to favor the group's members. Remember that the group's members are not the public.

Sure, most Realtors® want their sign in the front yard. And, for the record, I think it's fine to have a sign. Still, at least let the seller know the truth.

If you ever decide to get into real estate, you will hear about the three Ps. It's sort of a joke. It really isn't though, because so many agents seem to practice it. The first P: Place the home on the MLS and in the newspaper. The second P: Put up a sign. The third P: say a Prayer. Agents usually do say a prayer, but they'll never tell you that!

SOMEONE LOVES SIGNS

There is one type of seller who loves a For Sale sign in front of their home, and they're only 6% of all sellers: the FSBO. They don't want the help of a licensed agent, and are usually not in the local MLS. A sign really is effective when you don't have anything else that works.

> **SELLER MISTAKE**
> Thinking that a For Sale sign is going to help you sell your home.

BENEFITS ARE LIMITED

Much like having a landline phone, there are few benefits to having a sign in the yard. Many agents will tell you that not putting up the sign is like keeping your home a secret. Of course, for Realtors®, the For Sale sign can be an important generator of phone calls, similar in the way that an open house is an excellent way to get client leads and double-end a sale. (See Chapter 9!)

You've got to admit that a For Sale sign is convenient when driving to the property. Instead of slowing down to look at addresses, all you need to do is look for the sign in the yard. Bingo, we're here!

Always Be Closing applies to phone calls too. Agents want to "close" you, either by learning more about you, setting an appointment with you, or getting a lead from you. Most people don't want to talk to Realtors®, and I get it. They are scripted professionals trained to convert encounters into business. Many can be pushy and salesy. I'm not a big fan of agents either.

Still, we love phone calls because we don't get that many. We are trained to take advantage of every opportunity and "the sign" is one of those opportunities. When you call, expect the trained agent to say, "So, when do you plan to buy or sell?" We all sound the same because we've all been trained the same way. While we know that there is a small chance that you will buy the house you are calling about, there is a big opportunity to "work you" as a lead. Maybe you'll buy something, sell something, or know of someone who needs our help.

The target audience for a sign is a buyer who isn't using the internet. Maybe it's someone who isn't in the market to buy or a neighbor who isn't comfortable using the internet. A sign is essentially a billboard for the agent and their brokerage, announcing their services to anyone who drives by. It's also a great way to market yourself to the neighbors, much like an open house. Agents know that a neighbor is likely to sell soon, so they want their For Sale sign in your yard. It has worked for me.

PRIVACY CONCERNS AND UNWANTED VISITORS

Agents will usually forget to tell you the negatives of having a sign in your yard. But there are a few….

A For Sale sign tends to invite people posing as buyers onto your property and into your backyard. Some will walk right up to your door and knock. Homeowners who choose to install a sign might have to deal with the added risk factor of strangers asking to enter their home at random times. Who knows if they have any money, or if they've been pre-approved, let alone if they even are who they say they are?

When confronted, many will just say that they noticed the For Sale sign, and that they "just wanted to have a quick peek," or "I thought the house was vacant," or a number of other excuses. It doesn't happen often. It still happens enough that you should be warned.

If you're going to have a For Sale sign, then include a sign rider (a little sign on the For Sale sign post) that says, "Do Not Disturb Occupants" or "By Appointment Only." Having one or both riders can drastically cut down on those looky-loos.

Over time, the For Sale sign is being used less and less frequently. According to the most recent NAR Home Buyer and Seller Generational Trends Survey in 2021, only 68% of all home sellers said their agent used a real estate sign to market their home. But agents still like the sign. So do I, selfishly.

When REAL Trends conducted their most recent Real Estate Marketing Analysis Survey, they found that 80% of agents use real estate signs to promote their brand.

When I first started in real estate, I had my sign installed on every single listing. When Ms. Hauchbaum hired me for my first listing in 2001, I dug the hole myself. I was so excited that Anne took a picture of me digging the hole. That was in 2001, I was a rookie and I definitely wanted my sign in front of her house. Now I know the truth about signs and I explain it to my clients. Now, about half of my clients ask me to not put a sign in front of their house. I'm fine with that.

SOME PLACES GET IT

Have you ever noticed that in many resort towns, For Sale signs are not used at all? When my family vacations in Lake Arrowhead, it's nice to drive around the lake without seeing any For Sale signs. There isn't an ordinance that forbids signs; rather, it's an unwritten rule among the brokers that they won't put them up. Resort towns can have a tough time when the market goes down. However, when inventory is high, it can seem like the entire town is for sale. Those brokers know that the sign isn't that important and too many signs will hurt their marketplace.

Several predominantly wealthy communities are banning signs or restricting their size and location. For many of these communities, For Sale signs give a visual representation of how much inventory is on the market. A buyer driving down the street who sees quite a few signs might wonder why so many people want to move. Also, the For Sale sign can clutter the aura of the area.

The last time I checked, signs can't go viral, and they don't show up on Facebook or internet search engines. I often ask my sellers how a For Sale sign will attract an out-of-area or out-of-state buyer. Signs simply are not current technology. It's important to consider the number of people who will drive by your house every day and compare that to the way that homes are sold today: on the internet.

You want to sell your home. I get it. There is a compelling argument that you might as well do everything possible. You should at least know the good, the bad, and the ugly. My advice: hire an agent who tells you the truth about For Sale signs.

■ ■ ■

IS PRINT DEAD?

I think it goes without saying that print is dead … or is it?

As much as I love reading the newspaper, it's yesterday's news. These days, buyers rarely rely on print ads, mailers, or magazines to shop for their home. In 1981, 22% of home buyers read newspaper ads to search for real estate. That was before the internet. AOL started in 1985.

However, according to NAR, now overwhelmingly the first step buyers take in the home-buying process is to look online for properties (90%), and the next most common step is to contact a real estate agent. *Print ads and/or mailers aren't even in the top ten steps for selling your home.*

> **SELLER MISTAKE**
>
> Thinking that print advertising is going to help sell your home.

For years it's been disingenuous for your agent to tell you that they will aggressively market your home with print ads and mailers. According to NAR, a seller has just under a 1% chance of selling a home through print and mailers, combined. That number is likely to go even lower since the pandemic accelerated digital marketing. Sorry, but it is a failed business strategy to believe that your buyer is waiting for the newspaper to be delivered to get their home search underway. The stats have been creeping downward for decades. This is not how motivated buyers shop.

In 2020, NAR said the typical homebuyer was 47 years old and the typical home seller was 57 years old, and both parties say they use print to buy or sell a home less than 1% of the time. Let's face it, buyers are tech-savvy, and print is not going to help you sell your home.

Aren't you tired of getting real estate mailers? They're mailed in the immediate neighborhood of the listing, which is almost never where the buyer will come from. These pieces of paper are just advertising for the agent and their brokerage. I still send mailers out, and I do it every month. While I promote my listings and myself all the time, mailers rarely if ever generate calls about any of my listings. I mail stuff out because it generates leads for me.

All brokerages love to run print ads for the weekend real estate sections in newspapers. The deadline to get the ad in is the Tuesday prior to the following weekend, so by the time the weekend comes around, the listings are already at least five days old.

When I do encounter sellers who are convinced that print ads are important to sell their homes, it's almost always another agent who has convinced them. It happens when I am competing for a listing. The seller will tell me that the agent they interviewed before promised to place a lot of color ads, front page ads, and inside cover pages in the local paper and the *Los Angeles Times*. I have to smile and practically beg them to look up the stats.

While you might like the idea that your agent is covering all the bases, it takes an enormous amount of time and money to place these ads. Because it's less than 1% effective at best, you are better off asking your agent to put their resources into much more effective efforts.

BUT ADS STILL EXIST

As agents, we are constantly barraged by print media, direct mail, and printing companies to use their services. We all know, however, there is a minute chance of selling a home using print.

I still do have a small budget for ads. Almost every major brokerage does. There are several reasons for this, none of which will actually help the home seller. So why is the weekend paper full of print ads? Why do agents do so many mailings? Both must be working, right?

Other than advertising the agent and their brokerage, another reason is simply that everyone else does it. As straightforward and pathetic as that sounds, we just do not want to be the only brokerage in town that doesn't run ads. There is a considerable segment of the population that gets a paper and likes to look through the entire thing. But they are rarely serious buyers. Still, it's important for real estate companies to be in front of the reader. However, when the reader gets serious, surveys say they go overwhelmingly to the internet and ditch the paper.

The other reason is that sellers like to see their home in the paper. Even as a broker, when I sell my own home, I want to see it in the paper. I want to touch it, hold it, and pass it to someone. Hey, my house is in the paper! It makes me feel good, like I'm getting my money's worth. I want to be on the stage too, even though I'm in front of the wrong audience.

The fact is, we know that homeowners who are thinking of selling will look at the ads. They'll look for the list of open houses so they can start their research, or maybe they'll find a nice local agent to sell their home. After all, I get to market myself and the brokerage. That's about all that ads are good for. NAR knows this as well. Maybe that's why they combine print ads and mailers into one stat. Otherwise we'd be looking at fractions of one!

BAD PHOTOS AND A FLOOR PLAN

We've all seen bad real estate pictures. It's always disappointing, especially knowing that the seller is getting ripped off. Photography is one of the very most important parts of selling. The following may shock you. Almost all buyers look at the photos before reading the description—if they read it at all. You could say that buyers have mild ADD, or at least they behave like they do when they search for homes. Hundreds of studies prove that buyers take in information visually and if you don't have appealing and professional photos, then most buyers will click to the next property. What I've experienced for years is that listing agents rarely give buyers what's most important, which is part of the reason that I have been so successful.

Consider the following statistics from *Inman News*, the industry's leading source of real estate information. In an article they published called "Vast majority of real estate listings lack good visuals: Study," they reveal some startling facts. The following data resulted from an analysis of 25,000 U.S. listings from March 2021 to June 2021:

- 94% did not include a virtual tour (no 360-degree tour, no slideshow, and no video)
- 90% single-family homes did not include a floor plan
- Less than 30% used best practices in professional photography
- 67% of buyers want to see floor plans
- 58% of buyers want to see virtual tours

We know that most buyers stay online longer looking at your listing if you include a floor plan. Again, we are all visual. Give buyers what they want: photos and a floor plan, both of which simplify a buyer's decision to visit a home, speeding up the buying cycle. Let them feel what it's like to be in your house. After all, a home is a very emotional purchase, and it's so important to make a great first impression.

Pictures are THE most important selling feature.

Study after study has proven that buyers want to see good photos. The nicer the photos the better. According to NAR, 87% of buyers found photos to be most useful when searching for the home they purchased. Another study by VHT

> **SELLER MISTAKE**
> Not placing a big emphasis on the quality of the photos of your home.

Studios, the nation's largest real estate photography network for homes, says the use of professional photographs will sell a home 32% faster. Their analysis also shows the most experienced and productive Realtors® are typically the biggest users of real estate photography. Use of professional photography also delivers a higher perceived value, and a higher click-through rate by potential buyers. Yet so many agents don't spend the few hundred dollars to hire a professional photographer. If the photos aren't good (news bulletin: ALL cell phone photos are mediocre at best), your agent has blown it, and your potential buyer's attention will be drawn to competitor listings, quickly. Sorry, but if you're an agent who doesn't hire a professional photographer, then you're not acting as a professional agent.

SOME SCIENCE ABOUT PHOTOS

According to a *Wall Street Journal* article titled "20 Seconds for Love at First Sight," researchers found that 95% of buyers spend 20 seconds on the first photo on the MLS, and that picture should always be the curb view of your home. Buyers spend less than half of that 20 seconds looking everywhere else on the listing. How many times have you seen a horrible first photo on a listing? Does it entice you to look further?

Numerous studies have shown that after twenty-five images of the same property, less than 3% of your purchasers are still viewing your listing. I've found that twenty photos are more than enough for even large homes. The max should be twenty-five. If you have too many photos, the buyer might feel that they don't need to come to see your home. If you have too few, or don't have photos of important areas (like the kitchen or backyard), then buyers think that certain photos were left out for good reason. They may think to themselves that the kitchen must be in bad shape, or that the backyard photo wasn't included for a reason.

> **SELLER MISTAKE**
>
> Not using the most modern technology to feature your home in the best possible light.

One last word on this: **buyers aren't necessarily looking for a reason to see your home in person. Many are trying to filter out homes, trying to reject listings so that they can narrow down their search.** Giving them mediocre information plays into that buyer behavior. Give your buyers what they need to make the next move, not a rejection.

What About Drones, Video, and Virtual Reality?

Many times, a drone photograph can be advantageous. But there can still be drawbacks. They can show a neighbor's cluttered backyard, and even though a neighborhood negative could be hundreds of feet away, on a photo it can look so close that a prospective buyer will decide not to pursue your home. You may have too many trees. Some homes look smaller from a drone picture, especially if your neighbors' homes are larger. While transparency is important, sometimes too much information can be a hindrance. Not all homes are good candidates for drone pics. Drone photos can provide an extraordinary portrayal of the entire property. Getting these photos might cost your agent a few hundred dollars, but they are almost always worth it.

The recent pandemic has pivoted the real estate industry to incorporate more virtual reality and video, both of which have been with us for over a decade. These important tools make it easier to show a home, while also engaging more buyers to view it. Although video was used a lot prior to the pandemic, 3D virtual tours have now become more popular. A 3D virtual tour is a system of multiple photos taken throughout your home and digitally sewn together to allow a buyer to virtually walk through your property on their computer, at their pace. No headset required.

Virtual tours are more interactive and provide more information than video. You should expect every single top agent to utilize these technologies right now. If they don't, it's because they are afraid of technology, they're too cheap, or they're too lazy.

THE POWER OF A FLOOR PLAN

> **SELLER MISTAKE**
> Not providing a digital layout of your home to prospective buyers.

According to NAR, in 2020, the third most important feature buyers want is a floor plan, but the vast majority of agents do not provide one. Photos and property information were the first two items. A floor plan costs an agent just over a hundred dollars to create and can be digitized as a PDF or JPEG file, making it downloadable and easy to view.

It's unfortunate that very few listing agents provide one. I provide them for all of my listings and I am constantly being told that they were extremely helpful for keeping the buyer engaged online, while also encouraging them to make the decision to visit the house.

Homes that are better presented attract more inquiries. Buyers spend more time looking at them online. Great photos with floor plans get more looks, more looks generate more showings, more showings generate more offers, and more offers generate higher prices and better terms.

I often meet a lot of the buyers who have bought one of my listings. I am there during the buyer's inspections, when there's always a lot of downtime to chat. Invariably I will be told by the buyers that they liked the photos and were very appreciative that a floorplan was provided, and that my marketing got their attention and kept them engaged. I spend a lot of time picking the right photos, making the floor plan, and creating a virtual tour. It causes buyers to spend more time on my listings. It helps them to decide how they would like to live in the house and, invariably, to bid.

11

BE PREPARED TO FIRE YOUR AGENT

You've hired an agent and you are not happy. Your home isn't selling. There's nothing more frustrating in real estate than having a property that won't sell. As time goes on, things don't get better. What's even worse is when you can honestly blame your agent. Now that's a different conversation.

You want a fresh start with someone else who could bring the right strategy and new energy to the process. Waiting it out to the end of your contract is frustrating and inconvenient. Feelings get in the way. Can you imagine being in this situation with a friend or family member? Let's not go there.

Most people don't prepare for the worst. When the wheels come off, it's easy to look back at what you should have done. I hope that you aren't in this position right now. I do hope you've read through this book, including this chapter, because it has a lot of proactive advice that will make it easier to move on to another agent.

First, let's talk about being proactive, so you don't have to have painful conversations. Every year hundreds of thousands of homes do not sell. Most of those sellers didn't want that to happen, and I'm sure they were disappointed. Most homes do not sell because the seller made one or more of the mistakes outlined in this book. I have more than twenty years of observing it happen, which is why I wrote this book.

It's imperative to have a conversation with your agent at the beginning about getting out of your contract if you aren't happy. The most experienced, ethical, and successful agents will almost always agree to give you an easy-out agreement. An easy-out agreement is exactly what it sounds like. If the client is unhappy with the service provided, the agent will let them out of the contract, as long as there is open communication, and the agent gets an opportunity to remedy any situation that has upset the seller. Top agents don't make many mistakes. Remember that this is a relationship business. Agents want to maintain that relationship so it can lead to a sale, and to more leads.

Most agents won't offer this option, so it's important to ask about it. The way your prospective agent handles this part of the negotiation will give you a lot of insight into the kind of person you are about to go into business with to sell your home. It will give you a very good idea how your agent will behave if things don't go well.

> **SELLER MISTAKE**
>
> Not having an early conversation about how to handle problems later.

READ THE CONTRACT

The first thing to do is to read your contract carefully. Keep in mind that most real estate paperwork is comprised of standard forms provided by the local association of Realtors®. Therefore they are one-sided. Consequently, then, the bias favors the real estate agent in your area. Whether or not the form is a template, consider having an attorney review it. A local real estate attorney will be very familiar with these forms, and it won't take long for them to review. If your agent doesn't explain the contract, then at least your attorney will. Keep that attorney handy as you might need them later on.

BE A DETECTIVE

Whether your home has been on the market for one day or one year, you should act like a detective throughout the process. It's important to know what efforts have been made to sell your home. This only takes a few minutes. Google your address to see how your home is presented on the many online portals. Even if your home has been listed for a few weeks, the online views should be in the hundreds, if not in the thousands. Does your home at least have an easy-to-find dedicated website such as **www.123YourStreet.com**? You are paying your agent a lot of money, so it should.

Pretend you are a buyer searching for a home online and ask yourself if you've found enough information about the home that makes you want to take the next step. Check for basic and accurate information. This includes photos, price, square footage, and the phone number for your agent. Is the agent using bait-and-switch tactics? That means that the listing price or bed/bath count isn't available, thus requiring a buyer to call or email the agent for that information. Buyers hate this. The number one thing buyers want is information. They don't want to call a salesperson for it. Who does?

Are the photos second-rate? Are there enough of them? Are there too many? If you were a buyer, would your home look appealing to you? Do the photos show the home in its best condition? How do the photos compare to the homes that you are competing against? If the photos have been done poorly, or not at all, is that grounds for firing? Probably not. It depends on what else the agent is doing, or not doing.

Is your agent doing everything possible to market your home? There are likely clauses in your listing contract that stipulate the level of service you can expect. Does it seem to you that your home doesn't have the right type of exposure? Does it seem like competitive listings are easier to find and being exposed a lot more?

Is your home on social media? Was a Facebook campaign launched? The marketing and social media coverage an agent provides needs to be at least comparable to the other listings on the market with good exposure. You do want to stand out, don't you?

SELLER MISTAKE

Not checking on your own listing and making sure it is being well marketed.

Is your agent doing the things that benefit mostly himself/herself, or your sale? Are their tactics self-serving? Maybe you're not hearing from your agent at all, or not with enough frequency.

WHAT ARE THEY SAYING ON THE PHONE?

The way your agent handles a phone call speaks volumes as to how your sale is going to go. Agents have been known to say stupid things that actually dissuade buyers.

If your home is listed but isn't selling, and you have a feeling that your agent isn't on top of it, then consider having a friend pose as a buyer and call your agent. If your friend's call goes to voicemail, then consider how long it takes for a return call. This is a good way to show how friendly and helpful the agent is, and basically to find out how your agent handles a fresh lead. This will show how your agent handles their business, because most of the time the first serious interaction is over the phone.

When you left a message, were you called back? Is the agent scaring buyers and their agents away? Are they exaggerating problems with the home? The agent could be telling other agents (but not buyer inquiries) that the home is already sold (but it really isn't), so they can try to earn a double commission. If so, this might be grounds for firing the agent. The agent could be telling people the home is a tear-down when it is not.

Have a friend call the phone number to ask about the house and have them tell you what the agent says. Check to see if the agent says something like, "If you go through me, then you can get the house."

If agents don't return phone calls or emails, or they seem to always be on vacation, or too busy with their own lives, then there is a problem.

I get phone inquiries from dissatisfied sellers who are unhappy with their current listing situation about every other month. I can usually figure out what is wrong with the situation within a few minutes, just by asking four or five questions, and looking on the internet. Most top agents can do the same thing. If the problems are serious enough, you may have good cause to cancel a listing.

DON'T FIRE THEM. YET.

You might think I'm crazy, but whatever you find wrong, ask your agent to fix it. Ask for a new photoshoot, a floorplan, more marketing, a better description, more agent feedback and outreach, or more communication from them. Ask that they do not represent a buyer. Find out if your agent is offering a competitive and attractive buyer's agent commission. Some agents offer a below-market cooperating broker commission on the MLS. Since this is the last chapter of the book, I'll assume the other mistakes aren't happening.

Listen to your agent and see if their explanations sound reasonable. Give them a chance to improve the situation first. Maybe they had a family emergency, illness, or something they didn't necessarily want to share with you.

JUST ASK

Getting rid of your agent might be easier than you think. Simply ask your agent if you can be released. As my mom always said, "Just ask."

I've given this advice to a lot of other agents' sellers, and it works sometimes. Chances are, if you are hoping to switch agents, then your current agent may not want to work with you anyway. Maybe the agent has decided that your house will never sell. Maybe they've mentally moved on and are just waiting for the end date to come. Maybe they know they've done a bad job. Maybe they're tired of spending marketing dollars that don't seem to produce results. And, maybe they don't like you either. *If you ask, you might get what you wish for.* You may also get your agent to start working harder. You might also cause resentment. If that's the case, it's because you didn't hire a professional.

Sometimes personalities clash. Sometimes things don't work out. Usually, a homeowner and the agent can part ways amicably. In most circumstances, though, you cannot just call your real estate agent and tell them you want out and that you want someone else. It doesn't work that way with a contract.

Of course, some sellers want to cancel their listing because they want to renegotiate the commission. Maybe they want to list with a less expensive company or a discount agent. Alternatively, maybe they want to sell to a neighbor or friend and not pay a commission at all. Read your contract carefully as it is unlikely that these are valid reasons for trying to cancel.

Start by documenting what you are upset about. Whatever the problem is, the agent should be able to address it professionally. You should still put it in writing. The first step is to bring it up with your agent before going to their broker or manager. If it doesn't get addressed, then decide if your concerns need to be escalated up the ladder. If you have a good, experienced, and honest agent working with a reputable broker, they should be able to figure out the issues. When sellers are distressed about the sales process, agents will hopefully ask to have the chance to fix what can be fixed. Be sure to let them know what those fixes should be! An agent's goal shouldn't necessarily be to sell your home (although that is probably your ultimate goal). No, agents should want to make you so happy that you refer them to your friends and family.

Obvious justifications for firing your agent include fraud, lying, or other deceptive practices. These don't happen often, but consulting an attorney will help. For a few hundred dollars you can get the perspective of someone who understands contracts. An attorney who specializes in residential real estate will be the most effective and cost-effective choice.

Cancelling a listing needs to be done in writing. It's going to be upsetting when your agent tells you that they don't actually have the authority to cancel your listing. They need to get permission and a signature from their broker or manager to cancel. That's because the listing contract is with the brokerage. The agent is only the representative.

JUST WHEN I THOUGHT I WAS OUT … THEY PULLED ME BACK IN

You won't like hearing this: it isn't easy to get a brokerage to cancel a listing. In fact, it can be extremely challenging. It usually depends on the agent and how badly they want the commission. If the agent wants to get paid, they will ask their broker manager to fight for their commission. Often, both the agent and broker will fight (you) to keep it with the same brokerage. Many office managers will just refer the listing to another agent in the office, and that agent will pay a fee to your old agent once the listing closes. If the brokerage releases you, they might ask that you pay them upfront for their expenses, or they may ask your new agent to pay them a referral fee when your home sells. I'm not sure how that makes you feel. Sometimes sellers don't want their old agent to make a dime. I get it. If I were you, I'd tell them "Hell no."

Brokerage managers aren't all evil. They are usually reasonable. If you lay out your case, you will be much more successful than the person who yells on the phone (OR EMAILS IN ALL CAPS!!). Don't threaten legal action at this point. If it seems that the brokerage is unreasonable, then let them know you are going to call a real estate attorney. If you found an attorney, then let your brokerage know. If you have an attorney in the family who will work for free, let them know that too! Just don't make empty threats that you have an attorney and are going to sue. Maybe that comes later.

Let the brokerage know your reasons and intentions first—and do it in writing. Keep track of the actions that your agent didn't take or did not carry out professionally. If you don't get a reasonable response, or if you don't get a response at all, then it might be worth the time to have an attorney write a letter to the brokerage. This will get their attention. There's no guarantee, however, that a lawyer will get you the outcome you desire.

Even if you signed a long-term contract, you might be able to negotiate something shorter. If you are close to the end of the contract, you can just let it expire and you will be free to hire another agent of your choosing. This is a low-drama option that many sellers choose, but there are many issues to consider before taking it. Are prices going up or down? Are you headed into a traditionally slow period?

SELLER MISTAKE

Not being proactive when you are dissatisfied with your agent's results.

These days, buyers know how long your house has been on the market. The more time a home has been on the market, and the more agents you've hired, the more your property might be perceived as tough to sell. Also, you might be perceived as a difficult seller. Even though the reason for changing agents is poor representation, buyers and agents don't know this. They might think your house has problems if you go back on the market. I come from the school of fixing problems, even if it's tough.

I get a lot of calls from unhappy sellers, and I tell them all the same thing. If you can fix the issue right now, then you will probably be better off.

BE AWARE OF PROTECTION PERIODS

Another thing to keep in mind is that protection periods almost always exist in your listing contract, and these can be easily overlooked by the consumer. The protection period is the time period in which you will owe a commission to your original agent, even after your listing contract ends. It protects the agent's commission, not you. Just because you have relisted with a new agent doesn't mean you're in the clear. If you sell your home to someone who has toured the property while it was listed for sale with the original agent, you may have to pay a commission to your previous agent. Most protection periods are not terminated when you sign a new listing contract with another agent, so make sure to read the fine print. To validate the protection period clause, the agent is usually required to notify the seller in writing before the expiration or cancellation of the listing. Each state's association of Realtors® writes these clauses into these forms. Remember that the Realtor® associations are there to serve their members.

WHY DIDN'T ANYONE TELL ME?

Maybe you find yourself in a situation where everyone but you seems to know that you are working with an agent who isn't reputable. You ask agents their opinions, and they just tell you it's a tough market and ask you when your contract expires. No one will give you strategy, pricing, or market advice. That's because agents don't want to be accused of intentional and unlawful contract interference. Agents have to keep their mouths shut. Until you're out of your contract, it's usually up to you to figure it out.

No one wants to fire anyone, and no one wants to be fired. One of the best ways to resolve this common issue is to handle it in the initial interview, before you sign the listing contract.

A transaction isn't supposed to be a fight. I like to say that we all have the same finish line. Buyer, seller, agents, escrow, title, and lender all want to get over the finish line, and they have to do it together. However, mistakes can add up and we all get let down. Don't make the mistake of not being prepared for the worst.

CONCLUSION

Congratulations! You have increased your knowledge about selling your home, especially about the most common mistakes sellers make. Understanding why such mistakes occur is easier than figuring out how to improve the process, which is fraught with strong feelings, deeply embedded customs, and sometimes confusing information. As you've come to find out, the real estate industry isn't exactly on the side of the sellers. Agents often view sellers as lead generator tools and pawns for their own game, so it is up to sellers to make sure that doesn't happen. Few agents are willing to tell their clients about those mistakes—if they are even aware of their errors. Still, the truth is out there, and I did my best to lay it all out honestly using data, analysis, my experience, and common sense.

Since my first house sale on Marengo Avenue in Pasadena, I've learned from my clients' mistakes and my own. I have mastered effective selling strategies by avoiding errors I have outlined here, and streamlined the selling process. Unfortunately, I still see homeowners and their agents making those same mistakes every single day—mistakes that cost time, money, and headaches. However, you've read this book and now the odds are stacked in *your* favor!

Agents ask me all the time how I built my business. After a few minutes, I find that many really don't want to listen. They frown and disagree with me as soon as they hear that I insist on helping sellers before I consider the health of my business. The funny thing is, that position is what actually drives my success.

Going through this writing process has paid off. It has encapsulated what I've been doing and how I've built a successful business of repeat and referral clients. But, as you can see, it goes against the grain of our industry. I will admit that it made me a bit hesitant to write a book. I know I'll get some backlash. Thank you for taking this journey with me. I hope this book contributes to a louder voice for change.

THE TAKEAWAYS

1. *Interview at least three experienced local top agents.* Not doing this is the biggest seller mistake of all. Seventy-five percent of sellers interview only one agent. Having a tough time finding three worthy candidates? Call the manager at the large local brokerages and ask them to name their top agents. Ask your friends and do an online search. Do your homework to make sure your three agents have excellent reputations online and among their peers, and that they have a robust web presence. Check references. Search my website to see what a great web presence looks like.

2. *Don't give your listing away. Make the agent EARN your business.* Seventy-five percent of all sellers don't interview more than one agent. And 75% of all sellers don't use that same agent the next time to handle their transaction. Go through the principles in this book to find the agent who will do what's proven to get you the best price possible, and not use you as a business prop.

3. *Good is the enemy of great.* Have you ever had a good result and realized later (maybe years later) that you could actually have had a great result if you had done something differently? Too often, having a *good* agent can cloud your judgment and can

keep you from a *great* result. Hire someone great. He or she is out there.

4. ***Research your agents, and the homes they've sold.*** The agents, as well as the homes they've sold, should be easy to find on the internet. You should be able to find dozens, if not hundreds of homes they've sold. The way your agent markets their home listings is the way they will market yours. Look for professional photos, a floor plan, a property website, and a strong social media presence. Their home listings should pop up on dozens of real estate portals.

5. ***Think twice before hiring a friend or family member.*** Why mix business with personal relationships? If you have a loved one who feels entitled to sell your home, tell them you value the relationship you have with them so much that you would prefer to have a true business relationship with your agent—meaning, you would like the ability to yell at them or fire them if necessary. Business relationships work better when there is this sort of leverage. If you are going to make an exception, have Aunt Sue go through the interview process.

6. ***Favor a Realtor® with a broker's license and someone with at least five years' full-time experience.*** Experience is vital to a successful sale. Not all licensees are Realtors®. Most agents don't have a broker's license, which is harder to earn than a normal salesperson's license. Be careful hiring newbies. 87% of new agents leave the business within five years.

7. ***Teams and designations are impressive, but that's about it.*** Be wary of working with large teams. You will get passed around to multiple agents, some of whom will be newbies. Don't be surprised if you fall through the cracks. Successful agents with a small support team tend to be more successful and get more referrals and repeat customers than large teams. I certainly do. And don't judge agents based on the acronyms on their business cards: it doesn't always mean they are successful. It usually means they have a lot of time on their hands.

8. ***National and international firms have the best audience for your home.*** The larger the brokerage network, the larger the audience, the better exposure, which brings more buyers, more offers, and a better price and terms. The MLS is incredibly important. However, the brokerage's network is vital as well. Since no one knows where your highest-paying buyer will come from, it's important to have access to a large firm with strong tools, and a network and platform to market your home. Small boutique brokerages are appealing and cool, but they have smaller audiences, and fewer tools.

9. ***Technology isn't replacing the agent anytime soon.*** However, your agent needs to embrace technology. The use of agents has actually increased since 2000, and not even Wall Street thinks the agent will be replaced. Sellers continually say they need help with negotiating price and terms, determining listing strategy, advice about the selling process, and a dose of therapy. Technology can't do any of that.

10. ***Don't let your listing agent represent your buyer when selling your home.*** Understand dual agency and its perils. Dual agency rarely ever helps the seller. Keep in mind, it almost always benefits the agent and the buyer. Agents who want to do pre-marketing, bring in their own buyers, or do any open houses are red flags. Your agent should agree to be your advocate. The agent scores extra points if they voluntarily offer single-party representation within the first few minutes of the interview. It should be that important to you and to them.

11. ***For Sale by Owner.*** If you choose to sell your home yourself as a FSBO, understand the drawbacks of going it alone. Your home will likely sell under market value, with a heavy reliance on signs and open houses, a lack of marketing on the largest platforms, little to no liability protection, no access to the right forms, and you will be dealing with a variety of buyer types. *Ninety-two percent of FSBO sellers eventually list with a broker.*

12. ***Ask your agent about the Top Five.*** What are the top five positive selling points and the top five challenges of your property? Does your agent understand each of them? The positives should be the pillars of the marketing strategy, so listen carefully. Listen to how your agent will handle the most challenging aspects of your property as well. Agents blow sales all the time because they don't have clear, prepared responses to buyers' questions about a property's challenges.

13. ***Be sure to understand the market, pricing strategy, and absorption rates.*** The best agents will clearly explain the pricing strategy according to your marketplace and absorption rates. A great agent will get you market price, the best terms, and have a solid strategy to entice a bidding war. And yes, backup offers are always possible. If everything else is done correctly and you haven't sold your house, then the right asking price is the vital final ingredient.

14. ***Beware of "commission breath."*** You will know what it is when it presents itself. The most successful agents have a service mentality and aren't overly pushy. Get ample time to review the paperwork and make your decision. Ask yourself if the agent is trying to do it right, or just trying to make a sale.

15. ***If you can negotiate the listing commission, be careful.*** You are up against what is supposed to be a professional negotiator. If you can push around your agent, then so will everyone else. How the agent negotiates with you is how your home sale and concessions will get negotiated. Don't be offended if you can't negotiate the commission down. You get what you pay for.

16. ***Sell quickly, but not too quickly.*** The most and best buyers gravitate to a listing in the first few days. As time goes on, buyer interest (calls, showings, and web hits) slows down considerably. Selling in the first hours or days may cut out many of the best buyers and threaten the leverage of getting backup buyers. Each market is different, so find out if the best buyers come within the

first few days or weeks of going on the market. A quick look at comparables will tell you what's happening in your market.

17. **Don't let an agent "buy" your listing.** Agents can suggest an over-market asking price to win the listing, knowing there is little chance of getting your home sold. They'll just need to ask for price reductions until it sells, and chasing the market down is a slippery slope. It's a horrible strategy; don't fall for it. When a home is on the market for a long time it almost always yields fewer offers, lower prices, and worse terms. Dropping your price signals that you will negotiate and that you were definitely overpriced before. Also, showings do not always equal interested buyers—agents use overpriced homes to sell better-priced homes all the time.

18. **Don't rely on open houses.** Be wary of the agent who tells you to open your home to the public and who will do open houses until the house sells. NAR data shows that open houses are almost totally ineffective for the seller. The few benefits are monumentally eclipsed by the many problems an open house creates for the seller and their agent. Still, open houses have big benefits for the agent.

19. **A For Sale sign is ineffective.** A For Sale sign on a typical home has close to a 1% chance of selling a house. Signs also have the negative side effect of attracting people to your front door, to peek into your windows, or walk into your backyard unannounced. Signs are mainly free advertising for agents and brokerages.

20. **Print ads and mailers are almost useless.** Both are failed business strategies. Your first showing is always online. Most buyers will learn about your home through the internet. This should be the primary marketing platform, by far. Buyers are not looking in their mailbox or waiting for the newspaper to be delivered to shop for their dream home. Buyers say print has less than a 1% effectiveness rate. An agent who relies heavily on print ads and mailers is an agent who's more interested in marketing themself.

21. ***Professional photos and a layout are imperative.*** Buyers are visual, so give them what they want: great photos, the right number of them, drone photos, a digital floorplan and even a virtual tour. Your first showing is online. Don't blow your first showing!

22. ***Agent blues?*** If you feel that you've hired the wrong agent, act quickly to try to resolve the situation. Simply ask to cancel your contract. You might be surprised; they may not want to work with you either. Review the protection periods in the contract, and always consider speaking with a residential real estate attorney to review all your paperwork.

23. **One last tip:** Ask the agents you are interviewing about the principles in this book and see if they agree with them.

ACKNOWLEDGEMENTS

As I finish up this book, I want to give several Thank Yous to those who were a part of my journey.

My family was incredibly supportive, especially during the many evenings and weekends when I was hunched over my laptop.

I am most grateful to my wife, Anne. Thank you for riding with me on this rollercoaster of a career and allowing me to focus on this book, because you know how I can be distracted.

To my son Bradley, who introduced me to Graham Hurley, thank you.

To my other son Jettrin, thank you for constantly pushing me by asking, "Is your book done yet, Papa?" and reminding me to "stop watching *Breaking Bad*!"

To my dad and Malea, thank you for always encouraging me to aim high. I love you Dad.

To Mom and Ron, I'm glad we sold your home. It was a tough experience, and I learned a lot. Ron, thanks for teaching me all about construction. I love you Mom.

To my friend Wayne Grajewski, thank you for challenging me and for hiring me.

To Dave and Frances Valera, thanks for turning a light bulb on in my head.

To James Yu, my assistant, thank you for your help with this book and being on top of everything.

To my coach Steve Shull, thank you for keeping me on track.

To Jane Vander Velde, an English professor and client of mine, thank you for helping me edit this thing when it needed it.

To Linley Eathorne, another client who has written many books and offered to review this for me, thank you.

Thank you to my friend Jill Switzer, Esq. for the extra set of eyes.

Thank you to my manager Mike Williamson, for letting me bounce a lot of ideas off you, and to Tom Murray, who taught me the lesson of abundance in real estate.

Thank you, readers, for being interested in my first book. Honestly, I wish I had a book like this in my hands twenty years ago. This isn't my swan song. I probably have another thirty more years of selling real estate in me and maybe even another book. I love what I do, and I hope I've helped you. Feel free to contact me because, yes, I would be happy to help you with your home. If I'm not in your area, I am happy to find someone like me for you. You can find me at **www.michaelbbell.com**.

I wish you all the best,
Mike

If you enjoyed this book, learn more and get bonus material at **www.SellerMistakesTheBook.com**

DISCLOSURE

If your property is listed with a real estate broker, please disregard the information in this book. It is not my intention to solicit the offerings of other real estate brokers. You should always consult a real estate attorney and tax professional when selling real estate. Michael B. Bell holds a California Department of Real Estate broker license # 01164731.

NOTES